THE ONE YOU CAN BECOME

HAROLD ROGERS

ABINGDON
NASHVILLE

THE ONE YOU CAN BECOME

Copyright © 1978 by Abingdon

All rights reserved.
No part of this book may be reproduced in any manner whatsover without written permission of the publisher except brief quotations embodied in critical articles or reviews. For information address Abingdon, Nashville, Tennessee

Library of Congress Cataloging in Publication Data

ROGERS, HAROLD, 1907–
  The One you can become.
  1. Christian life—Methodist authors. I. Title.
BV4501.2.R642   248'.48'7   78-17127

ISBN 0-687-29199-2

The quotation on page 23 is from "Vestigia" from *Poems* by Bliss Carman. Reprinted by permission of Dodd, Mead & Company, publishers, and by special permission of the Bliss Carman Trust, The University of New Brunswick, Canada.

Scripture quotations in this publication unless otherwise noted are from Today's English Version of the New Testament. Copyright © American Bible Society 1966, 1971.

Scripture quotations noted RSV are from the Revised Standard Version Common Bible, copyright © 1973.

Scripture quotations noted Phillips are from The New Testament in Modern English, © J. B. Phillips 1958, 1960, 1972.

Scripture quotations noted KJV are from the King James Version of the Bible.

MANUFACTURED BY THE PARTHENON PRESS AT
NASHVILLE, TENNESSEE, UNITED STATES OF AMERICA

For our grandchildren
Robert and Andrea

PREFACE

God is only a thought away. The writer said, "Come near to God, and he will come near to you" (James 4:8).

Try it! The first beneficiary will be yourself. You will have unexpected adventures where you thought life was humdrum. You will make new friends, experience a zest for living. Fear of failure will be changed by the anticipation of success. God has plans, not problems for our lives.

Did not the Master Teacher say, "The Kingdom of God is within you" (Luke 17:21)?

The kingdom of God is God's great answer to the world's desperate needs, collectively and individually. Not many people deny God, they just ignore him and that is equally bad, for to do so is to ignore the greatest force in the universe. Many fail to experience miracle-working power because God requires faith that leads to obedience.

When we open the door to God to let him expand our lives, three things happen:
- We learn to have total confidence in the Master Planner of the universe.
- We listen carefully to his directions for us.
- He endows us with a new source of strength, love, understanding, enthusiasm.

A great basketball coach whose teams won ten N.C.A.A.

THE ONE YOU CAN BECOME

titles said, "If we execute our fundamentals as we are supposed to, then we should win."

So it is with life.

The only difference between those who find wholeness and those who are torn with anxiety, doubt, and failure is the pattern of their thoughts. When we were created in the spiritual image of God we were given the freedom of choice—dependence on the spiritual, the force that wins and that is our only true independence, or dependence on the physical, which at best is only temporary and too often leads to futility at the end of the road.

That there is a vast hunger, an impoverishment of the spirit, few will deny. Perhaps because of our involvement in the tangibles we have relegated God to a future time and place, forgetting that all things rest on the spiritual here and now and that the only real strength we possess comes through our union with the Power who is as close as our next breath. For too long we have forgotten that his Spirit dwells within us and that we must recognize and accept his omnipotence (all power), his omniscience (all wisdom), and his omnipresence (everywhere).

When we are out of harmony with God, we are out of harmony with our neighbors, our families, and ourselves. We have missed the fact that the New Covenant had completeness for its theme. Jesus proclaimed it when he said, "Whoever drinks the water that I will give him will never be thirsty again. The water that I will give him will become in him a spring which will provide him with life-giving water and give him eternal life" (John 4:14).

To drink of this water we turn inwardly to our secret place, as Jesus calls it, thereby charting our destiny, for the truth is that the outer life is but a reflection of the inner thought. More than anything we need to remind ourselves that we are spiritual beings with all the power we need to achieve wholeness for life at its best.

In his book *How the World Began*, Helmut Thielicke has

PREFACE

written, "Once God has become the theme of man's life it becomes exciting."

Because as I open my life to God I am finding this to be true, I hope to share something of this sense of excitement with my readers.

H.R.

CONTENTS

A World Divided   15
Who's Knocking?   21
The Question   30
Prodigals   36
The Force That Wins   41
About-Face   48
The Command Post   56
To Work Miracles   63
Our Heritage   70
A Divine Plan   75
Good Judgment   82
Prosperity   88
Healing   95
Stand Firm   103
The One You Can Become   108

THE ONE YOU CAN BECOME

A WORLD DIVIDED

It was an ordinary noon luncheon with ten of us gathered around a table, until one member of the group said, "I want to give you folks an attitude test. In one word I want each one of you to tell what your attitude is at the present moment." There was an uneasy silence, even some nervous laughter, then one by one the words spilled out. Different! Yet not too different. In retrospect they added up to attitudes of anxiety, caution, hatred, bewilderment, confusion.

Intrigued, I followed up on an individual basis. When I asked one of the number, a man well established in the financial world, he said, "It's understandable. We live in a world divided. We are constantly concerned with power, military might. Our slogan seems to be peace through strength. Yet the words of the ancient prophet are there to haunt us, 'Not by might, nor by power, but by my Spirit, says the Lord of hosts.' (Zech. 4:6 RSV). We are trying to straddle two kingdoms, the kingdom of materialistic might and the kingdom of the Spirit."

I talked with a woman whose name regularly bylines feature articles and whose marriage of twenty-four years had ended in a messy divorce. "Yesterday, at the luncheon . . . "

She interrupted me. "You thought I sounded bitter. Well, I am. There is one little trollop I could cheerfully throttle with my bare hands and go to jail for it if necessary."

THE ONE YOU CAN BECOME

"Maybe," I said, "but there's got to be more to it than that."

She snubbed out a cigarette. "We've done some very wonderful things in the name of the Master Teacher who taught us the greatest thing in the world is love. We've built churches, hospitals, schools, libraries; written books, hymns, poems, but there is one thing we have neglected to do, live a life-style in harmony with divine reality. We live with hate, greed, jealousy, anxiety, fear, and I'm just as bad as the next. Sure, I believe in God, but I've made these other things a part of my life until I've perfected them. Do I shock you with my forthrightness?"

"No. Only the puzzle grows deeper," I said.

I talked with a minister of a large metropolitan church. He said, "Of course there's confusion. Just to give you an illustration, by pushing a button in a certain place we send men to the moon, then we push another button and bring them back to earth, but we haven't solved the problem of loneliness. In my church I have some thirty-five or forty members who haven't a living family member. They are lonely, frightened. They say, 'Suppose I have a stroke or become helpless, where do I turn?' But they aren't alone. Look at our teen-agers. Many of them feel completely rejected. We are told that Jesus was acqainted with grief, but that isn't an answer that satisfies the widow sitting alone in a low-income housing project or a teen-ager with alcoholic parents or one whose friends are putting on peer pressure to indulge in sex and drugs."

A university professor said, "Certainly I am confused. Some of us are educated beyond our intelligence. We know more than we understand. Too often we become real cynics."

My next stop was an editor's office, a man of a different race. He said, "Yes, man, I'm glad you came. We talk about brotherhood. Some of you even refer to me as Brother in the right group, but could I move into your neighborhood and feel comfortable? Would my family be accepted the same as anyone else? You don't need to answer that." He forced a smile. "Somewhere we've missed the boat, haven't we?"

A few days later I was to talk with a judge. In the years he has been on the bench he has presided over cases involving almost every kind of human tragedy—divorce, child abandonment, purse snatching, rape, murder.

He said, "Somewhere we have failed to come up with a true sense of values. During the past fifty years we have made tremendous strides in scientific research and invention, yet the lag between physical science and the science of person-to-person and person-to-God relationship is our major problem today.

"Perhaps to escape from our dilemma, even for a few moments, we are witnessing an overemphasis on vacuous entertaiment, sensuality, even brutality. Only too well we should know from history the debilitating effects of such a course on ourselves and upon civilization."

Jesus said, "The eyes are like a lamp for the body. If your eyes are sound, your whole body will be full of light; but if your eyes are no good, your body will be in darkness. So if the light in you is darkness, how terribly dark it will be!" (Matt. 6:22-23).

Did Jesus really say that? And if he did, did he mean it as it sounds?

As I pondered that statement, together with the answers I had received, I became convinced that he meant it exactly as it was stated. That being the case, the big question became to whom and in what direction do we look for the solution?

I recalled that the late Dr. E. Stanley Jones made the statement that the majorty of us gaze at the world and glance at Jesus when in reality we should be glancing at the world and gazing at Jesus.

Like the others at the luncheon, however, I had to live in the world, use its money, drive on its highways, travel in its airplanes, shop in its stores, abide by its customs. The world was my life, or so I argued.

But wait a minute! Jesus lived in the world of his day. Were we, and specifically was I, letting the world cast a shadow between me and my best? And were those shadows causing dark places in all of our lives? Often accused of being a heretic, Jesus lived in the light of God's love, and the accusations caused not a moment of hesitation on his part. When there was a choice to make, and frequently there were choices for him, he made his decisions only one way. He said, "My food . . . is to obey the will of the one who sent me and to finish the work he gave me to do" (John 4:34).

That thought stayed with me. It captured my imagination. When something captures the imagination we focus all of our attention on that one thing. When I was writing western stories, even though I lived in the West, I became not just an avid reader but a student of the master western writers. I wanted to capture something of their style, their methods of handling certain situations. If I could learn from those writers, I wanted to learn.

To be captured by an idea is to want more and more knowledge about it—to make it part of our lives. We wake up thinking about it, we go to sleep and dream about it. We talk about it, read about it until it becomes uppermost in our minds and is imbedded deep within our subconscious, and finally is a living reality.

Suddenly I found that Jesus had captured my imagination. I wanted to know more about him than I had ever before known. I wanted to think about him, read about him, and follow him as much as it was humanly posible to do. Just as a youth wants to follow his baseball or football hero, the young musician wants to follow the master of his or her particular instrument, the young artist spends long but happy hours with the paintings of the particular artist who in

A WORLD DIVIDED

a real way is setting the tone or life-style for him or her, so I wanted the Christ Spirit to set my life-style.

Having settled in my own mind that there was nothing unnatural about living in the world and facing up to all of its challenges, yet wanting to follow the Master Teacher, I began in earnest to discover everything I could about him. I read the four Gospels with a searching, probing mind, not just once but several times. Eventually this led to the rest of the New Testament and finally the Old. In Paul's letter to his friends at Corinth he said, "Surely you know that Christ Jesus is in you?" (II Cor. 13:5).

At first I did not get the full impact. I read it again, and it jolted me back on my heels. Jesus Christ in any human being, but especially in me? The divine Son of God in me with all of my shortcomings, the temptations I lived with and to which I yielded, my fits of anger, my desire for revenge, my fears, the various little gods I had set up as goals.

I said, "Now, Paul, you wrote that to folks who lived two thousand years ago, not for those of us living in the twentieth century." Still my knowledge of human nature told me there hadn't been too much change in the intervening years. We still have to deal with anger, lust, covetousness, envy, greed, and hate just as they did in Paul's day. If that were true when Paul wrote then it was still valid.

Still I wanted to kick the idea around a bit longer—Jesus Christ in me! I didn't want to go off on a tangent, be a kook. I had seen too many ride one religious hobbyhorse for awhile, then change saddles in the middle of a bounce. I continued searching, probing, meditating, praying. I needed help.

When I raised the question with some people, there was a moment while they followed along, then tactfully changed the subject. Of course there were a few, but not too many, who asked where I got the idea in the first place. When I said, "It's in the Bible," one person retorted, "Oh come now, just because it's in the Bible."

THE ONE YOU CAN BECOME

That was just it—there it was in the Bible with reference after reference. Jesus had said, "The Kingdom of God is within you" (Luke 17:21). At another time he said, "Whoever loves me will obey my teaching. My Father will love him, and my Father and I will come to him and live with him" (John 14:23).

Cautiously, very cautiously, even secretly, I began to take those statements at face value. When certain situations developed I reminded myself that the Christ Spirit was in me. It did make a difference in my actions and reactions. Even though others might not know it, I did. Oh, not all the time. Lifetime habits are not that easily changed.

Because I teach a rather large adult Sunday school class, mostly business and professional people, and conduct numerous workshops and seminars, I began interspersing some of those thoughts into my teaching. At first I was careful to disguise them or hurry over them, but little by little I became bolder in my assertions. "The Kingdom of God is within you." Or, "Surely you know that Christ Jesus is in you?"

Then the questions began to come. "Why haven't we heard more on this subject? Do you really? Do you really believe it? Honest now, do you? Did Jesus and Paul really say those things?"

To all of their questions I responded, "Yes. Absolutely yes."

WHO'S KNOCKING?

Before too long I discovered that we were failing to catch Christ's signals, and there was one signal the majority of us had missed entirely. For some reason we have held to the idea that it was we who were knocking on God's door to get his attention so that we might voice our requests. If we could only discover the correct position, say the right word when we were praying, we would be more successful, and most certainly if a group of us were together to really put on the pressure there was even a greater chance that he would respond.

However, our Lord didn't explain it quite that way. He said, "Listen! I stand at the door and knock; if anyone hears my voice and opens the door, I will come into his house and eat with him, and he will eat with me." (Rev. 3:20).

When I pointed that out, a grandmother in the workshop exclaimed, "That really blows your mind doesn't it? Like Job, we've been running around saying, 'Oh, that I knew where I might find him,' when all of the time he's been standing on the front steps waiting for us to open the door."

A Muslim mystic once said, "I looked for God for thirty years. I thought it was I who desired him, but no, it was he who desired me."

Perhaps one of the differences between ourselves and saints like Brother Lawrence, John Woolman, Thomas Kelly, Hannah Whitall Smith, and E. Stanley Jones, to name but a few, is the fact that they were constantly aware of God's presence in their lives and were ready to follow his slightest whisper. The inner voice speaks to the whole person, saint and sinner alike, if the ears are attuned to hear it, and is not reserved for the intellectual or the monk in the cloistered cell. It is for all who will listen and follow. Thus we strive to give more and more of our individual attention to him and his eternal order. As we look at the Master, we discover that life as he lived it is more than a religion, even more than a way of worshiping God; it is a way of dealing positively with the daily challenges of life while giving free rein to God to work in and through him.

Too often, however, we have thought of God in terms of religion only, to be met in the sanctuary or during our times of prayer, thus we have placed on him limits he never intended. If all we know of the presence of his Spirit is that which we experience in these moments of so-called devotion, we are short-circuiting the Life of life, for it is "in him we live and move and exist" (Acts 17:28). From him we are constantly receiving life. His presence is great enough for the whole universe, yet individualized enough for each one of us to be in union with his infinite Spirit.

Really, it matters little what we call this presence—the Inner Light, the Divine Presence, the Universal Mind, the Holy Spirit, or the Infinite Spirit—so long as we accept his presence and supremacy. For me, however, it is the Spirit of God or the Christ Spirit. I find it hard to love a Universal Mind though some of my devout friends have no trouble at this point. Rather I prefer to think of God, the Father, as exemplified by Jesus when he said, "Whoever has seen me has seen the Father" (John 14:9). I can and do love Jesus Christ, because I can to some extent visualize him, but I cannot visualize a Universal Mind; it seems as cold and impersonal as a computer that has me completely baffled.

I can visualize and experience our Lord because I see his autograph on ever sunset, every sunrise, on every flower and shrub, on every person.

WHO'S KNOCKING?

Bliss Carman wrote:

> I took a day to search for God,
> And found Him not. But as I trod
> By rocky ledge, through woods untamed,
> Just where the scarlet lily flamed,
> I saw His footprint in the sod.

In his Letter to the Romans, the apostle Paul wrote, "Ever since God created the world, his invisible qualities, both his eternal power and his divine nature, have been clearly seen, they are perceived, in the things that God has made. So those people have no excuse at all" (Rom. 1:20).

In his *Institutes of Christian Religion,* Calvin wrote; "God revealed himself and daily discloses himself in the whole workmanship of the universe. As a consequence, men cannot open their eyes without being compelled to see him."

Yet the doubter insists that God no longer makes himself known to us as he did in Bible times.

Here I always ask, "What do you mean, in Bible times? In so-called Bible times there was no Bible. Now we have the Scriptures, both the Old and New Testaments. We have the advanced knowledge of science, once thought to be an enemy of Christianity, but that now confirms daily the reality of the unseen. We have the witness of those who have experienced this Christ Spirit in their lives. And we have the indwelling presence, the still small voice that communicates to us even though we may have muted it by trying to call our own signals. What do you mean, God no longer reveals himself to us? If only we would listen and follow this voice within our own souls by acting in accordance with it we would do the right thing, in the correct manner, and at the proper time."

It was after I had given this response to a very vocal skeptic in a workshop that another member of the group said, "I think it might be helpful if you would tell us how you

THE ONE YOU CAN BECOME

personally hear this voice of which you speak with such assurance."

To that one I am indebted just as I am eternally grateful for those who have a way of coming directly to the nub of the question and holding the speaker or writer to the nitty-gritty.

For me it has become almost routine. Each morning when I awaken I begin by stretching and feeling an awareness of all parts of my body. I say. "Thank you, Lord, for watching over me throughout the night and bringing me to this new day." Physically as I move my feet, my legs, my arms, my body, my head and shoulders, I thank God for giving me this physical structure that has served me so many years. Then in gratitude I offer myself to him to be used as he wishes. With this matter cared for, I quickly review the plans for the coming day, asking him to guide and direct me and to keep me open for any directions or changes he may wish to make in the hours ahead. I want to be receptive to the hidden possibilities he may see in the day I am about to begin.

These are also moments to realize our uniqueness and our opportunity. This is the time to let the Christ Spirit in us help us to grow to our full potential. Age does not enter in as we come to realize our true worth and to let the peace and the excitement of the indwelling presence of the living Christ fill these moments with expectation. This is the time to realize that we are children of God, and that as such we are important to him, to others, and to ourselves.

During the months I have practiced this habit I find it easier to turn to him several times throughout even the most demanding day, a practice explained in a former book entitled *A Handful of Quietness,* and to be aware of my union with him even though I may be rushing to catch a plane or am involved in a spirited discussion.

At night, upon retiring, I follow a similar routine. As I relax my body, member by member, I thank him for the care and life he has given to every nerve and cell of it. Mentally I review the events of the day. If I have made mistakes, I ask for forgiveness and for the wisdom to correct my shortcomings. If there have been highlights during the day, I thank him for those and ask for a peaceful night with his angels keeping watch over me and all of those who seek this guardian presence.

During those occasions when I find that sleep does not readily come, or when I awaken in the middle of the night, I begin by thanking him for the rest and renewal I am experiencing as I allow the bed to support my body. I tell him that I am ready to listen if there is something I should hear and understand. Occasionally during these moments, when my world is softened by darkness, I do feel the stirring of ideas that will be put to use at a later time. More often than not, however, the quietness of listening is the antidote for sleeplessness.

If there is some part of my body that is hurting I say, "Lord, you made my body. You know every bone and muscle, every nerve and artery in it. Surely because you made it you can repair and restore any part of it that is not functioning properly. I trust you for that. If there are changes I need to make in my physical, mental, or spiritual habit or if I need to seek other help, I am open for your direction."

These times, just as in all times of prayer and meditation, are moments to be perfectly honest with God. He knows us and understands us far better than we understand ourselves. We need not try to magnify or gloss over our mistakes or make any rash promises we will not keep in the days ahead. He knows we are not perfect, so in open honesty we come clean by turning to Jesus Christ for forgiveness and liberation. In so doing we become aware of the kingdom of God that is within each of us, this divine center from which we move freely and creatively into the externals of life with the full knowledge that the great requirement is for us to recognize him and respond to him with faith and obedience. We do not pray or meditate to change God. Rather these are the times when he communicates to us that which he proposes for us so that his will may flow through us and out into his universe.

While we will all admit there is a vast difference between bowing to a spiritual principle in the sanctuary and living it in the thick of daily life, the great central fact in our relationship with God is that we become aware of him only as we open the door of our souls to his indwelling presence. Still, if we are honest we know that too often he disappears from our vision.

To make his presence a living reality we must consciously respond to his summons over and over again until it becomes as natural as breathing, a subconscious action on our part. Consciously we know that God is peace, that he is love, beauty, the source of all good, happiness, health, prosperity. He is life, the very heart of all we think and do and are. Consequently we must begin to think of him, not as way off out there somewhere, but as deep within, a very present reality.

In a vague way we may know that we are the temple of the living God and that we are two bodies, a spiritual and a physical. For the most part, however, we are aware primarily of the physical, for we are conscious of being hot or cold, hungry or tired. These demand top priority. They refuse to be ignored. The defeated ones despair, "Life is too much for us." But what life are we talking about, the physical or the spiritual? And do we have the wrong idea of what true life really is?

Here we are again forced back to Jesus' statement, "The Kingdom of God is within you." (Luke 17:21). The kingdom of God—that personal relationship between the divine and the human—is present in every one of us!

In reality we are talking about both the physical and the spiritual that constitutes total life, not a life in which they are separated, but a life in which they are one beautiful whole.

WHO'S KNOCKING?

We are talking of a life of peace and joy and trust, where we release all of our desire to him, yet at the same time accept responsibility for those things that are our obligation. Again, not easy.

So we look to him for our example. There was the mortal part of Jesus, the part that hurt, became tired, hungry, thirsty, wept, but was also joyous, the welcome guest at the wedding feast. This was Jesus, the Son of man, but there was also the Son of God—Christ, the anointed One. Just so each of us has two beings, the one that says, "I cannot take another step," and the other that says, "With his help I will."

The One who created us did not wind us up like a spinning top and set us to rushing about until we are out of energy to drop and rise no more. God not only created us in the beginning, but he is ever present to supply our needs. Over and over again Jesus tried to instill in us the idea that the same God, the same source of energy and inspiration available to him, is also available to us in the here and now.

He told us so pointedly that God was "the God of the living, not of the dead" (Matt. 22:32). Over and over again he emphasized the fact that he and God were one, that without God working in and through him he could do nothing. Never once did he tell us that this relationship was reserved for himself alone; rather he said it was available to every one of us if we would but open ourselves to such a relationship. He said, "I am telling you the truth: whoever believes in me will do what I do—yes, he will do even greater things" (John 14:12).

This, perhaps, is one of the most exciting statements in the Gospels. It should stand out in boldface type when we consider the possibilities it promises for those who have the necessary faith. To heal, to touch, to point humanity in the true direction, this is within the realm of all who truly accept the words of the Master Teacher.

Deep down in the center of our being we find the true

THE ONE YOU CAN BECOME

Spirit of the living God; yet if we give free reign to the Spirit, the Spirit does not remain there inactive. The very presence of the indwelling Christ flows into every nerve and fiber of our being, taking with it life and energy and health. We could not exist, even for a moment, without this presence that we so casually accept and carelessly ignore, this presence that Augustine decribed as "most hidden, yet most present."

In "Every Man Is King," H. Emilie Cady has written:

> There is a great difference between a Christian life and a Christ life. To live a Christian life is to follow the teachings of Jesus, with the idea that God and Christ are wholly outside of and, to be called upon but not always to answer. To live a Christ life is to follow Jesus' teachings in the knowledge that God's Indwelling Presence, which is always life, love and power within us, is now ready and waiting to flow forth abundantly, aye, lavishly into our consciousness, and through us to others, the moment we open ourselves to it, and truthfully expect it. One is following after Christ, which is beautiful and good so far as it goes, but it is always very imperfect, the other is letting Christ, the perfect Son of God, be manifest through us.

Evelyn Underhill expresses this idea so well in *A Journey with the Saints.* "The mystic allows himself to become filled with God's Spirit; and once full of God's Spirit of power, love and wisdom, he pours out this Spirit on his fellow-men. Thus their lives are bettered because he has become an instrument of God's Spirit."

Paul was so convinced of this that he said, "Christ is in you, which means that you will share in the glory of God" (Col. 1:27).

The writer of the Letters of John expressed something of the same thought: "Because the Spirit who is in you is more powerful than the spirit in those who belong to the world" (I John 4:4).

Again the ones in the workshop ask, "How? Tell me how."

In her concise Quaker fashion, Hannah Whitall Smith has

WHO'S KNOCKING?

given direction in her book *The Christian's Secret of a Happy Life.*

It is a very simple transaction, and yet very real. The steps are but three:
We must be convinced that the Scriptures teach this glorious indwelling of God.
We must surrender our whole selves to him and be possessed by him.
We must believe that he has taken possession, and is dwelling in us.

THE QUESTION

In Luke's Gospel there is the dramatic account of the blind man who came to Jesus crying out for help. In response Jesus asked a direct, but simple, question using nine one-syllable words: "What do you want me to do for you?" The man answered, "Sir, I want to see again." Jesus said to him, "See! Your faith has made you well" (Luke 41-42).

It was a question and an answer not limited either by time or circumstance. Today, as then, Jesus is still asking the same question of every one of us, "What do you want me to do for you?"

Individually we are to make our requests known to him in faith, believing. Before making our request, however, we need to think it through carefully. If it is only for selfish reasons, or if by the granting of it another would in any way be harmed, then because of his nature, Jesus cannot grant it. Nor would we expect him to do something that we can do for ourselves.

Actually there are no limits on prayer and its results providing our requests are consistent with the nature of our Lord. At this point Jesus insisted on a very definite ground rule: "If you remain in me and my words remain in you, then you will ask for anything you wish, and you shall have it" (John 15:7).

Here Jesus is explaining that we cannot have a hidden agenda. Everything must be open and aboveboard.

THE QUESTION

With the blind man there was no question. For him the greatest gift in the world would be to receive his sight. Without hesitation Jesus granted his request.

In Mark's Gospel there is an equally thrilling account of a healing. A father came to Jesus with a son who suffered from seizures, and pleaded, "Have pity on us and help us, if you possibly can!" Jesus said, "Everything is possible for the person who has faith." The father cried out, "I do have faith, but not enough. Help me!" (Mark 9:14-24).

When the Lord appeared to Solomon in a dream and said, "Ask what I shall give you," Solomon requested understanding so that he might govern wisely and discern between good and evil (I Kings 3:3-15 RSV).

To restate the question "What do you want me to do for you?" in a group where there is participation is a wide-open invitation to spirited discussion and oft-changed answers if there is time enough for individuals to honestly come to grips with the enormity of it.

A young mother, with a fast-crippling illness, said, "For me there is no question. I only want healing until my children are able to care for themselves."

Hands were clasped. There were prayers that the presence of the living God would heal the one whose request seemed so natural. And before too many days there was a decided improvement, not a total remission of the illness, but significant change for the better.

In another situation, an unemployed electronics engineer whose wife was working as a waitress in a restaurant to support the family said, "All I want is a job. We're six months behind on our house payments. We've sold our boat and one car. Just give me a job where I can use my experience and support my family, and I'll not ask for anything more. Everywhere I go it seems the doors are closed. I've about given up."

There were a few sympathetic comments, then one man in the group said, "Ben, the labor market is tight, but you do have some outstanding qualifications, and somewhere there is someone who needs what you have to offer. Perhaps you have tried until your own attitude of discouragement is defeating you. Supposing you just begin to picture all that you have to offer, and at the same time know there is a place for you, then really let go and let God bring it about?"

Ben shook his head. "I have prayed, but there have been no answers. Sometimes I wonder if I believe anything."

A blonde teen-age girl in sandals, blue jeans, and a T-shirt with block letters that read, "Don't follow me. I'm lost already," exclaimed, "More than anything I want to be understood and trusted. My folks are always saying to my sister and me, 'You kids better stay in line. You get caught smoking pot or get pregnant, and you'll regret it as long as you live.' We haven't smoked pot, and we haven't gone all the way. Sometimes I want to swim out in the ocean and just keep on swimming."

A woman in the group said, "No one is happy who lives under a cloud or suspicion and harassment, yet there may be an answer. I hope you won't reject it as being too pat. Paul, in his letter to his friends at Rome, wrote, ' "If your enemy is hungry, feed him; if he is thirsty, give him a drink; for by doing this you will make him burn with shame. Do not let evil defeat you; instead, conquer evil with good' " (Rom. 12:20-21).

"That doesn't say a thing to me," the girl retorted.

"No, I suppose not," the woman said. "But let's interpret that to fit the occasion. If your parents are impatient with you, be patient with them. Don't let their suspicion upset you. Tell them you love them and trust them and that you're not going to do anything to cause them worry or unhappiness."

"You think it would work?" he girl asked.

"It's worth a try," the woman said.

In another group a woman said, "I've been praying that

THE QUESTION

my husband will become a Christian. So far my prayers haven't been answered."

When asked why she wanted him to be a Christian, her first response was so that he would be easier to live with.

At that another member of the group asked, "Has your husband seen anything in your life that would make him want to be a Christian?"

There was an uncomfortable silence until she finally stammered, "Why I suppose there are a number of things. I'm a good housekeeper. I'm not extravagant."

"Do you nag at him to become a Christian?" the questioner persisted.

"Well, of course I try to get him to go to church with me."

"But have you demonstrated to him what a Christian life can mean in a family?" another asked.

"I'm not on trial," the woman stormed.

"Oh, yes you are," a man in the group said. "We're all on trial everyday, where we live, where we work, where we play. You said the reason you want your husband to become a Christian is so he will be easier to live with. Is that the only reason?"

"Of course not."

"What are your other reasons?"

"If he were a Christian he would be here with me instead of objecting to me coming."

"Did he object?"

"He threw a fit. He always does."

"Did you leave some good food for him for while you are away?" another woman asked.

"There's plenty of food there if he wants to fix it."

"But he'll have to fix it?"

"Well, excuse me. I didn't know there was anything wrong in wanting your husband to be a Christian, but apparently there is."

The next morning she was the first to speak in the group. She said, "Last night I couldn't sleep. I kept thinking about some of the introductory statements, 'The kingdom of God, the Spirit of God, the presence of God, is within you.' If that is really true, it's for sure I haven't let it show in me. I guess that's what I really want—to let God's Spirit show in my life. It isn't going to be easy, but that's what I want."

A few days later I was to share some of my experience of the past weeks with an attorney, a man who is also a retreat leader.

"I hear you loud and clear," Dave said. "They are all legitimate desires, but you know something? There is a good bit of the prodigal in all of us. We want the gift, but we don't really want the Giver."

"Come again," I said.

"All right. Take the man who needed the job. Did he just want a job, which would be the gift, or did he really want to make God a part of his life, to let God guide him, and to be committed to God? Was he willing to admit that God is the source of all good, all health, all prosperity? If he got a job, would he have learned anything from the experience, about financial planning, and about giving? We want the gift whatever it is—love, understanding—but was that teen-age girl ready to let the living Presence become a part of her life until her parents knew it? There's a bit of chicanery, the old Jacob, in all of us until we've wrestled the whole night through. And sometimes it takes more than a night. It may take a lifetime.

"In the Sermon on the Mount, Jesus said we were to give first place to his Kingdom and then he would provide everything else for us. When we really and truly seek him he will provide. His very Spirit is within each one of us. His is the most powerful force in the world if we only rely on him."

"You sound as if you're making a plea to a jury," I said.

"Could be."

I was preparing to leave, but Dave motioned for me to remain. "The other evening I picked up one of my kid's books from an English class and read the part where Sir

THE QUESTION

Galahad said, 'My strength is as the strength of ten because my heart is pure.' Jesus said, 'Happy are the pure in heart; they will see God!' (Matt. 5:8). To see God, to experience the living presence of God in our lives, isn't that the real answer to the question, 'What do you want me to do for you?' When and if we do that won't we have everything we need?"

I said, "Dave, let me answer you by telling a very real experience. Some years ago I was on a speaking trip in Texas. There was a custodian in the church where I spent several days. His name was Wakefield Jones. He had experienced most of the trauma that a black man would experience before any real progress had been made that would affect him, yet he had something that had pastor as well as parishioners going to him for help. I heard it almost from the moment I arrived. I wanted to know his secret, so I went to him and asked. That's the only way I know to get answers. He leaned on his broom and smiled. 'The Lord is my shepherd, that's all I need.'

"I asked him to write his name in my Testament. He did, and after it wrote, Ps. 23:1."

PRODIGALS

It is a haunting question: Do we truly want the Giver (God), or do we only want the gift (our desires)?

In Dante's descent into the Inferno he found his path to the Mount of Joy blocked by three beasts of worldliness. They were the leopard of malice and fraud, the lion of violence and ambition, and the she-wolf of incontinence or lust.

A young woman in a group discussion said, "Of course I want to be a committed Christian, but I'm always faced with the question of what I may miss if I follow the path of self-denial that some of you are suggesting. Right now I find life so exciting I guess I'm selfish at this point. You see there are so many things I want to do, I've already made plans. Probably I just don't have the necessary faith to turn my back on some of these things, or perhaps I don't really know what faith is. I wish someone would tell me."

To her question concerning faith a businessman responded, "Faith is trusting God to keep his word. It is thanking him for his presence in our lives and attaching ourselves to him." Then he added, "In Genesis 8:22 you will find these words, 'While the earth remains, seedtime and harvest, cold and heat, summer and winter, day and night, shall not cease.' If we had no other promise this one should be sufficient cause for us to trust our Creator."

As the discussion continued a woman in the group said, "Perhaps the first step we need to take is to really think about the words of the psalmist, 'Be still, and know that I am God' " (Ps. 46:10 RSV).

"Until we pause and realize that God is omnipotent, omniscient, and omnipresent, we are prone to remain the do-it-yourself kind with all of its inherent problems. To try to make it on our own is to reject the help that is available to us. At that point we are prodigals; we want our fun, but still have the opportunity of turning to God for help when life caves in, when in reality we need God's help and wisdom all of the time. We need to give him the opportuntity to change our plans, our actions, and our attitudes if he has a better way."

To become still is to find the Christ Spirit within us, that moving force that sustains, strengthens, enables. We remember that at the very beginning of time God said, "Let us make man in our image." (Gen. 1:26 RSV). Very shortly thereafter God reviewed all that he had made and declared it "good" (v. 31 RSV).

To be created in the image of God is the gift that has been given to us, a gift too often forgotten. It is in our quietness that we discover the image of God that is in every one of us rather than just to live in the mere shell of our physical body. What a tremendous thought—the Spirit of the living God is in each one of us if we but let his Spirit become evident.

As we come to appreciate this more fully, we are gradually enabled to let go and let God take over, to take over the impatience, the willfulness, the scheming. If we have felt that we have to fight and connive to attain some desired goal, we may discover that we truly do not desire such an attainment, but that there is a better way to achieve our ambition—God's way. Again we look at the prodigal and see ourselves.

The author of *The Imitation of Christ* wrote, "My son, says our Lord, always commit your cause to me, and I shall dispose of it well for you, when the time comes."

Again, and once again, we remember that we are more than just mortal beings even though the physical appearances seem to be a hard fast reality. We are spiritual beings before we are physical beings, and as such we have the freedom of Spirit. Problems cannot defeat us. Our future rests not in us alone, but in the Power of powers—God.

When we are open to the force within, our sights are lifted from problems to possibilities. Every one of our needs, our problems, are a matter of our Creator's concern. His presence eternally surrounds us and moves in according to our faith and need. Always we hold fast to the knowledge that whether we are asking for ourself or for another, God is hearing our requests and is acting on them in the manner that is best for all concerned.

To direct our attention to the perfect good is to see past the immediate to the greater life in God. We may not see it all at once. Our problems may not be solved as quickly as were some of the problems we read about in the Scriptures, but there is a solution though it may require patience. This may be our greatest need, the thing we want our Lord to do for us—give us patience.

Here, perhaps, we need to enlarge upon our idea of faith by realizing that faith is always positive, never negative. Too often by our actions and attitudes we cancel our prayers with more reality than we pray them.

To illustrate, we pray for health but decide even before going to a doctor that the pain in our body is cancer because several members of our family have died from cancer. We pray for a job, but in all of our conversation discuss the shortage of jobs and the large number of unemployed until our efforts to find work are only half-hearted. We pray for prosperity, then say we don't know where the next penny will be found. Time after time we are betrayed by our doubts. We have such complete faith in the negative that we never doubt our doubts.

We have programmed our minds so ardently with the negative that our first step on the road to a vital, living faith is to reprogram our thinking, our conversation, our actions,

PRODIGALS

with a positive approach by affirming, "I am a new person. I will think only positive thoughts. There is only good awaiting me as a result of God's presence in my life."

A young man who had spent years of hard work to become a musician suddenly developed a health problem requiring drastic surgery that brought his plans down in a heap of rubble. There were some bad days, yet he was never comletely defeated. He had an inner strength that caused him to affirm, "Someday I will wake up, and things will be different."

One day, while he was still in the hospital a friend asked, "Did you ever think of becoming a music librarian?"

For him it was the opening of a new door. True it meant more hard work and sacrifice, but the end result was a new career in which he found happiness.

Never think that Jesus, when he walked the earth as the Son of man, was an impractical idealist expounding a set of moral precepts that were not livable. He was a practical realist giving direction for life as it could be and not as it may appear to the majority of us. His life and words were an outstanding example of faith in action, trusting the final outcome entirely to the Father's supreme intelligence.

Too many of us are prone to say that the things he advocated will not work in today's world, but in all honesty we do not know, for we have never tried them. While we may try to live outwardly in accordance with the commandments of God, inwardly we stumble in darkness as we live by the senses rather than by the true Spirit of the indwelling Christ.

Such changes as the one proposed will not be instantaneous. For too long we have filled our minds, our subconscious, with negative ideas. Every negative thought we have had is stored in the inner recesses of the subconscious ready to spring forth at the most unexpected moment to cause us to waver and doubt. Do not be dismayed or become discouraged when that happens.

THE ONE YOU CAN BECOME

Rather say, "This is the old me thinking, not the new." Then counteract it with a positive affirmation.

Nor do we think of our Lord as a far-off and unapproachable potentate sitting on a throne issuing orders to his subjects in an impersonal manner; neither is he keeping a ledger of our deeds ready to deal out our rewards or punishments. He is a living friend coming to us, holding out his hand, looking into our eyes, walking in our shoes. We do not need to go to some distant shrine to find him. Wherever we are he is. Our troubles, our pains, our joys, are his, perhaps even more than they are ours, though he is not as baffled by them as we often are. He has a ready answer and is only waiting for our acceptance of it.

By ourselves we are not equal to life, but with him we are not only equal, we are victorious. Our first step is to realize our own inadequacy. The second is to know that this power and guidance are available to us. Finally we see ourselves as channels for his life to flow through us and out into the universe.

What has been described as the kindest promise in the Bible are the words of Jesus when he said, "Come to me, all of you who are tired from carrying heavy loads, and I will give you rest" (Matt. 11:28).

William James, the well-known psychologist, has said, "The turning point in religious experience is self-surrender."

Here a good prayer might well be, "Thank you God for giving direction to my life. Today I open myself completely to your presence."

Pray it. Live it.

THE FORCE THAT WINS

In his book *A Touch of Wonder,* Arthur Gordon has written, "Love life, so that life will love you."

There is a retired schoolteacher living in our apartment complex who might well have been the inspiration for that sentence. In her apartment she has a few antiques, some beautiful blue dishes, pictures she has selected, and shelf after shelf of books. That is her home base, but by foot, by bus, and with friends in their automobiles she is constantly exploring and finding happy adventures in everything and everyone that she gladly shares with all those with whom she comes in contact.

For her roadmap to life she must have read the old monk in *The Brothers Karamazov* who advises his followers: "Love all of God's creation, the whole and every grain of sand in it. Love every leaf, every ray of God's light. Love the animals, love the plants, love everything. If you love everything you will perceive the divine mystery in things."

If her life is an example, love is the force that wins, for she loves and is loved like sunshine after a stormy night. If we are rich when we love, then she is one of the richest persons in the world.

There is no true measure for the impact of love, but its results can be felt, seen, and enjoyed. Yet love can also mean pain, for when it is blocked or trampled upon, it can bring anguish. Consequently love is not without an element of risk. Still love does no count the cost, rather it enters into a full participation of life and lets the still greater love of God work in and through us.

Love and electricity have a great deal in common; we don't really know what either one is, yet we constantly see what each one can accomplish. We are tempted to say there is a bit of magic in both, and perhaps there is, except the most ordinary people enjoy them or are hurt by them without any hocus-pocus.

If God is love, then love is untrammeled by time or space and waits only for us to become a channel for it just as a strand of copper wire is a channel for electricity. Nevertheless, there is only one way in which true love can be used—constructively.

In Jesus' two great commandments the key word is "love"—love for God and love for our neighbor (Matt. 22:37-40; Mark 12:30-31; Luke 10:27).

Again, it is so easy to read about love and give lip service to it, but so difficult to truly live. How does one love the unlovely, the one who has brought hurt to us, even taken our mate? Humanly it is impossible; spiritually, if we meditate upon the words, "For God has poured out his love into our hearts by means of the Holy Spirit, who is God's gift to us" (Rom. 5:5), then and only then can we let the Christ Spirit in us respond.

When we are the recipients of an injustice we are prone to be critical of the one or the situation causing our hurt. It is only as we pray and meditate that we begin to have peace of mind and heart and are able to have a new outlook. If there is something we can do to overcome the injustice we will be given direction. If there is nothing we will remember that so long as the indwelling presence remains within us we are never alone, never defeated. Prayer and meditation will help us to handle the experience constructively.

Many years ago a very wise teacher counseled, "Always begin with yourself. If you cannot love yourself how can you

THE FORCE THAT WINS

love another?" For her key she quoted, "God lives in union with us, and his love is made perfect in us" (I John 4:12).

More often there are those times when nothing really traumatic has happened, still we feel a sense of restlessness and dissatisfaction. We wish that we were someone else or somewhere else. Perhaps the daily routine has suddenly become sheer drudgery. We may feel so insignificant, even unwanted and unnecessary.

Here we need to pause and look at ourselves. Who are we, really? If only we would let God's love work in and through us right where we are, imagine the tremendous opportunity that is ours and how the world about us might be changed.

Love is more than a sentimental emotion; it is our attitude toward life, it is reverence for all of life, even ours.

And so we begin with self. How many of us beat ourselves over the head with past mistakes and shortcomings? Jesus never told us not to love ourselves. Rather he said that we were to love our neighbor as ourselves. If this be true, if we have a very low opinion of self, then we cannot do too much better for our neighbor.

When we think of love we tend to think of our feelings for others, and we may think of the end results rather than the beginning. While it is good to think of God's love in terms of the entire universe so far as we are concerned, as individuals it begins with us. We are the channel of love. God loves us, therefore we love.

As we bring harmony into our own lives by realizing God's love is a very part of our own being, we find our thoughts becoming actions. We meet the problems of life from the center wherein God's love dwells in each one of us. The acceptance of God's love brings light to those areas of darkness, doubt, and fear. We are uplifted.

Love, true love, is that magic gift with no return demanded. We hope, but we do not demand, for love is unselfish; it brings its own rewards, because love, like faith,

THE ONE YOU CAN BECOME

is always positive. We then discover that as we develop a divine love attitude, we help others in doing the same. As this blessing of divine love spreads from person to person our world assumes a different hue. We discover that which we send forth does come back to us.

To love is to share, to give and to receive, to be rich with an inner peace and fulfillment. Love is the greatest treasure in life. Physically? Yes, but so much more. It is that divine meeting of spirits that all eternity will not erase; it is the mortal and the immortal. Rightly directed it knows no limits, yet love does not seek for self alone.

All of us are spiritual beings. We can either be good spirits or bad spirits. We can either have the Christ Spirit radiating from us or a negative spirit sending out its vibrations. The world will either be better for our having been a part of it, or it will be damaged because of that which we have or have not shared. Whether it is going to be a spirit of love or a spirit of hate, whether it is going to be a spirit of good or a spirit of evil, depends upon our receptiveness to the love of God and the light that he shines through us. It is so important for us to become aware of and to understand the possibilities we have.

We receive strength and direction as we open ourselves to the indwelling Spirit of Christ. Whenever we close ourselves to it we make mistakes and falter. We become persons of darkness rather than persons of light, and those persons who come into our lives are affected by the nature of the spirit that dwells within us. They are influenced by us either for the positive or the negative depending on where we are in this regard when our spirits meet. Even to pass a person on the street where the contact is only momentary affords an opportunity for spirit to meet spirit. This often overlooked principle can, and does, work miracles that make it so important for us to be aware of the indwelling spirit of love in our lives.

How do we learn to love? We learn to love by accepting

THE FORCE THAT WINS

God's love. We only become givers as we become receivers. As we move through the day with all of its varied activities we remember that God's love lives in us and that we have asked him to use us as a channel to give expression to his love. Here we recognize another principle; it takes time to love, and it takes effort.

When we make ourselves available to him in this way we must be willing to let go of every unloving thought or feeling that would hinder the flow of such love. When we harbor resentments, thoughts of revenge and retaliation, our inner peace is disturbed. We are living in the negative not the positive. In that state of mind we are first of all hurting ourselves. We are not being true to self. The indwelling Christ, the very best that is within us, can think only positive thoughts. If we continue to be disturbed by the negative we say, "Thank you, God, for living in me." This positive statement outweighs the negative. When we think of his presence, our thoughts become harmonious, but because inharmony may have such a hold on us we may have to come back again and again to thank him for living in us.

Love, by its very nature, is freeing. It releases us from that which has held us in bondage. Love does not ask, Who deserves love and who does not? Love is the harmonizing principle of the life of the individual, the family, the neighborhood, and the universe.

Because God is love we cannot contemplate him without thinking that he loves others as much as he loves us. For the moment we may question how he can love the one who has wronged us so, but God breathed the breath of life into that one just as he breathed it into us. We are both God's creation. His Spirit indwells within all of his creation.

A woman, standing by the casket of her husband who had died an alcoholic, said, "At heart he was such a good man. I loved him."

Everyone knew the heartache, the deprivation, she had suffered because of his habit, still she had lived with him for

THE ONE YOU CAN BECOME

more than a quarter of a century and borne him three children, because she loved him—not an easy love, but an undying love. No doubt that woman hated her husband's addiction to alcohol with every ounce of her being, but she loved him and stood by him even in death, which was caused by the habit that had shackled him so many years. Somewhere along the way she had learned the great secret of love—to forgive.

When we have been hurt by someone we have a choice to make. We can harbor that hurt deep within, or we can turn to the Christ within and do as he would have us to do, instantly forgive. When we learn to do that we have freedom.

To have physical freedom is something we all crave, but to have spiritual freedom is true freedom where we feel at one with the Christ, at one with our neighbor, but best of all at one with ourself. It is through his spiritual freedom that we find our oneness with every facet of life.

"Get rid of all bitterness, passion, and anger. No more shouting or insults, no more hateful feelings of any sort. Instead, be kind and tender-hearted to one another, and forgive one another, as God has forgiven you through Christ" (Eph. 4:31-32).

Forgiveness is the costly part of love, and sometimes it costs so much. Were it not for the fact that God forgives, there would be no hope for any of us. Consequently as we accept his forgiveness and love we pass it along to another, trusting him for direction. When we recognize his presence and his love, we feel loved and are happy. We love because he first loved us. Jesus demonstrated how to live—in short how to deal with the negative emotions of fear, hate, guilt, jealousy, and replace them with the spirit of love, thereby making our lives victorious here and now and to continue through all eternity.

Love is the way to the Kingdom. Jesus knew it and led the way.

THE FORCE THAT WINS

A PRAYER FOR EVERY DAY

Father, whose life is within me and whose love is ever about me, grant that thy life may be manifested in my life today, as with gladness of heart without haste or confusion of thought, I go about my daily tasks conscious of my ability to meet every rightful demand, seeing the larger meaning of little things and finding beauty everywhere. In the sense of thy presence may I walk through the hours, breathing the atmosphere of love and seeking by love rather than by anxious striving to quicken and bless the lives of others.

Knowing that I am a fellow worker together with thee, may I live above everything that tends to depress or discourage and finally come to that assurance of faith which is itself the victory that overcometh the world.

And now I would enter into the secret place of thy presence, that hidden in thee my soul may be refreshed with a sense of thy sheltering care and all my energies quickened into newness of life. In Jesus' name we ask it. Amen.

—Source Unknown

ABOUT-FACE

Of all the barriers we erect between ourselves and our own good, our spiritual power, one of the most difficult to overcome is an unforgiving spirit. It defeats us at every turn as long as we harbor it. It robs us of health, prosperity, and friends. It divides families and causes inefficiency in those places where we work. It short-circuits our prayers to God. Dwight Moody underscored this in his preaching. He said, "If I regard iniquity in my heart and am not willing to give it up, I need not pray, for there is no room in my heart to receive the blessing I seek." He compared it to taking a bottle, corking it up tight, and placing it under Niagara Falls, where not one drop of water from that mighty falls would ever enter the bottle unless it was opened.

Consequently our first task is to recognize this unforgiving spirit for what it is, an insidious enemy to ourselves, and deal with it by decisive action, remembering that the forgiver always takes the initiative.

Here a very apt illustration comes to mind. Two longtime friends were pheasant hunting. It was a windy day, and the birds were not getting up well. Finally a big cock literally exploded from beneath a clump of weeds directly behind them. Both men whirled and fired, the one on the left just an instant ahead of his friend on the right. The bird crumpled and plunged to the ground. As the man on the left, who had shot first, stooped to pick up the prize, the other man said, "I believe that pheasant belongs to me."

ABOUT-FACE

The argument that ensued was most bitter. A third member in the party who had been hunting a bit to one side, yet had witnessed the whole affair, tried to bring about a settlement only to be met with angry words. So bitter was the argument that the bird was finally left where he had fallen.

For more than two years those two men didn't hunt together. Then one day, the man who obviously had shot first telephoned his old friend. "Bart," he said, "I have a new gun. I think the stock needs some work to make it handle better. I wonder if you would go out with me and try it?"

After a long pause Bart said, "You know I will Cal. I have a new dog. I'd like to have you see him. I'll bring him along."

Every season from then on those two men hunted together until Cal died. He left his gun to Bart, the man who had shot last but insisted the bird was his.

Perhaps one of the most needful prayers we can pray is, "Lord teach me how to forgive myself and others."

In reality, forgiveness is the gift of God working through our souls. As long as we concentrate on the imperfections in ourselves or in others they will multiply, but when we truly forgive we shift our focus to the good.

When others fail to measure up to our own self-made rules so often we become judgmental, we criticize, even reject. We make ourselves and those around us miserable. To practice an attitude of love and forgiveness sends out vibrations that lift everyone and everything, even plants and animals, to a higher level. Both the giver and the receiver benefit. An ancient philosopher said, "Love tempered with wisdom is the secret of life."

Almost without exception our first target should be the enemy within—self. Right here there are two great lessons we need to learn: the first is that God loves us, and the second is to behave ourselves. Knowing that God loves us we are able to forgive self, and to behave ourselves is to stop flaying our minds with the memory of past mistakes

THE ONE YOU CAN BECOME

and be willing to start anew with a life-changing experience. For too long the majority of us have been carrying around thoughts of past failures, times when we have not lived up to our best, and so we learn to release from our minds all negative thoughts of self and to radiate the Spirit of Christ who dwells within each one of us.

There are those who feel they have failed a loved one who is now gone from this earth by not doing all they should have done and as a result live in constant misery. Others are clinging to the bitter shreds of a failure in school or business, a broken marriage. Many feel they have been a failure by not measuring up to the standards expected of them by family and friends or by failing to attain certain goals they have set for themselves.

No matter what our mistakes and disappointments have been, or how we may have thought of ourselves, we catch a new vision of our possibilities. We see ourselves as God sees us, created in his image. We begin to think of self as one of his children, forgiven and redeemed with the only limits being those we place upon ourselves. We overcome the habit of judgment and condemnation by directing our thoughts to the inner perfections rather than the outer flaws.

Because God is love he does not deal in failures. He did not create us as a failure or misfit. He breathed the breath of life into our bodies. He created us for wholeness and to fulfill a worthwhile purpose. He sees us for what we can become if we are open to his direction rather than what we have been or are at the present moment. Having the Spirit within us, we have the possibility of becoming confident, helpful, victorious persons capable of the greatness he planned for each one of us. He has made us eternal, spiritual beings to carry out some particular task that only we can do, small though it be.

Long, long ago God said: "I will forgive their iniquity, and I will remember their sin no more" (Jer. 31:34 RSV).

Therefore we begin by affirming, "God has forgiven me, I

ABOUT-FACE

forgive myself. He is with me right now, helping me to do an about-face."

With that prayer we put ourselves in his hands and trust him to remove all of those negative thoughts and actions that are hurtful to us and to others. We empty ourselves of the negative, making room for his Spirit to enter our lives.

No longer do we depreciate self. The old has passed away, the new has come. True, we may learn from our past mistakes, even use them as a springboard for our leap of faith. The initial leap comes as we begin to have a sense of union with God and feel our own pettiness and selfishness begin to disappear. This may be the first appearance of the tangible evidence for which we have been seeking.

Before we begin dealing with our relationship to others it cannot be emphasized enough that to hold feelings of resentment, jealousy, spite, the desire for revenge or to make someone suffer, is to bring more suffering to ourselves. The hater is invariably hurt worse than the hated. It surfaces in so many ways and when we least expect it. Consequently, for the sake of self we desire to be freed from it. We release and are released.

Dwelling upon old grievances mentally, seething over how badly we have fared because of another, has the effect of keeping alive that which should have expired from neglect. To harbor resentment of any kind is to keep us in bondage to that from which we would be free. Total forgiveness is the most freeing action we can take.

What really matters is not what has happened to the outer person; it is the inner person, the Spirit within, that counts. It is not the actions of others, but our own inner thoughts in that secret place that make or mar our lives.

A woman attending a workshop admitted that she was carrying the deepest kind of resentment toward a stepdaughter who was threatening her marriage. She said, "I simply can't like or forgive her because I do not trust her. She would knife me in the back at the slightest opportunity."

THE ONE YOU CAN BECOME

Deep-seated feelings such as that cannot be dismissed with a wave of the hand or even some magic words, but it was suggested that she borrow some words from the ancient guidebook, "I will bless you . . . so that you will be a blessing" (Gen. 12:2 RSV).

That idea was then enlarged upon by suggesting to her that when the old bitterness welled up, or a feeling of distrust, she should form a mental picture of the one who appeared to be a threat to her and affirm, "I will bless you . . . so that you will be a blessing."

She was advised to repeat that prayer again and again until there came a time when she could add, "I forgive you because the Spirit of Christ is within both of us." For it is only as we place our confidence in the Spirit of Christ that these disturbing appearances disappear and become a blessing to one another as the poison is counteracted by a spirit of love.

Rather than trying to batter a barrier down physically as we would attack a stone wall with a sledgehammer, we begin reaching for the presence of God that flows into our lives and from us into the lives of others. We do not look at the negative attitudes we have allowed to exist as we realize the one against whom we have felt resentment also has the indwelling Christ within his or her life. We begin by keeping uppermost in our minds that this same Spirit within us can and is contacting the Spirit within our bitterest enemy, and that it is the spiritual, not the physical, that breaks through the barriers. With the Spirit there are no insurmountable barriers, no walls that cannot be penetrated.

If a disappointment has come to us we do not resist by asking, "Why me?" We realize that the eternal nature of God is for good and that with his help good can come from the most bitter experience. We do not allow ourselves to indulge in self-pity, needless questions, or recriminations of any kind.

In the Scriptures we are admonished that we are not to

resist evil. By no means does this mean that we are not to try to overcome evil with good. Rather it means that we are not to rebel against it.

One of the first lessons a boxer learns is to roll with the punches. By rolling with the punches we mean to stop the damage before it has been inflicted. When another is being difficult we spiritually back away from it by centering our thoughts not on the outer but on the inner person, the Spirit of Christ that is in both of us. Very often to concentrate on that in a quiet fashion not only stills the emotions that are threatening to surface in ourselves, but it will have a most astonishing effect on the one who is causing the difficulty. Very often the troublesome one is uptight due to a cause of which we know nothing. To retaliate in kind, as we are often tempted to do, will only compound the misery. Instead, at the first sign of storm clouds we switch our thoughts from the physical to the spiritual. A little practice will work wonders.

Consequently if someone has said something unkind about us, something that hurt feelings or would damage us if we allowed it to, we immediately forgive him or her. We say it was just the outer person speaking, not the inner, spiritual person. When someone has betrayed our trust, rather than hold a resentment we begin with forgiveness. If there is unfairness on the job or in the home, it is so easy to become bitter and live in an unhappy state. There is no harmony in this. To enjoy any semblance of harmony we begin by affirming forgiveness rather than discussing or thinking about the unpleasantness.

Because, for too long, our reactions to the negative have been negative, we tend to make excuses for ourselves by saying, "I would be a hypocrite if I said I could forgive and forget when I cannot." Here we would remember that the first order of heaven is forgiveness. If that were not so, the majority of us would not have a chance. One cannot conceive of heaven without recognizing that forgiveness is

THE ONE YOU CAN BECOME

the rule and guide. Just as forgiveness governs heaven, so it should manifest itself in the affairs of human relations. If one's thoughts are filled with bitterness and resentment, only confusion and disharmony can result.

Having been a part of the average life so long, negative thoughts will come unbidden to the mind during those unguarded moments. They literally grip us and rend us unless we remind ourselves of the unchanging forgiveness of God and that his Spirit is filling our lives at the present moment. By turning our attention to the indwelling Christ we realize that within the secret place we are one with him. We remind ourselves that with him the past is gone, all we have is the present moment. If we have him for the present that is enough. With him we learn to live in the now, forgetting the past and knowing that we can trust him for the future. We say with the one who had suffered so much, "You will forget your misery; you will remember it as waters that have passed away" (Job 11:16 RSV).

Another focus of our resentment is often an organization, a political party, or even a particular race of people. When it comes to issues, of course there is polarization. That is only natural, yet despite our differences of opinion, or even life-style, we can live with this division without bitterness when we realize our unity in Christ is greater than any outer differences we may have.

The apostle Paul stated, "So there is no difference between Jews and Gentiles, between slaves and free men, between men and women; you are all one in union with Christ Jesus" (Gal. 3:28).

When differences arise, as they will, this should be our first thought, our oneness with the Christ through his Spirit that indwells within.

Whatever the cause of our negative attitudes we need to throw off the mental bonds that have held us for too long by affirming forgiveness and oneness and accepting liberty. Just as we personally accept God's forgiveness, we remember that all of his children must be accorded the privilege. Because he forgives and accepts, we too must forgive and accept, realizing that when we do there will be a restoring of all things to harmony and wholeness. There is a sudden burst of joy when we are freed of failure, guilt, envy, resentment, inferiority. It is the breaking of bonds that have shackled us to the past, and suddenly we are released for all of the possibilities God holds in store for us. It is only in complete forgiveness that we achieve maturity of the soul.

This cannot be emphasized enough. It is useless to expect true happiness, health, or prosperity as long as we cling to anything contrary to the nature of God. To realize the total good that can be ours we must forgive and accept forgiveness without reservation.

We forgive.

God forgives.

There are no limits.

The Christ Spirit living within will help us to see beyond our differences and look into the goodness in the heart of every individual if we open to such a leading.

THE COMMAND POST

In *Paradise Lost,* Milton wrote:

> The mind is its own place, and in itself
> can make a heaven of hell, a hell of heaven.

The philosopher said: "Be careful how you think; your life is shaped by your thoughts." (Prov. 4:23)

Paul wrote: "Let God transform you inwardly by a complete change of your mind" (Rom. 12:2).

To put it quite simply, if we would be different persons, if we would alter our lives, then the first step is to change our thoughts, for our minds are the greatest creation on earth. The mind controls us, but conversely we can control it with practice and discipline, because thought patterns are subject to change. Actually the kingdom of God (the peace and joy and serenity and love of God that we talk about) begins with our thoughts. This is where we shape our destiny. In fact it is the whole of life, for the outer person is but an expression of the inner. We become the visible expression of our own invisible thoughts.

A convict, serving a long sentence for a vicious crime, said, "Don't talk to us about rehabilitation until you have talked with us about remotivation. We've messed up, but help us to catch a vision of the one we may become."

A large request, but large requests demand large answers.

THE COMMAND POST

Paul, writing to his friends at Corinth, said, "We, however, have the mind of Christ" (I Cor. 2:16). Such a statement staggers the imagination. You and I, that convict behind prison walls, can have the mind of Christ! How?

First we get a vision of the one we may become by forming a mental picture of Jesus, not how he looked physically, but how he met temptation, how he responded to challenges and troublesome situations, what happened to the people who were touched by his life: the woman with the issue of blood, the man with the withered hand, the thief on the cross, the disciples. Was it the things he said, or was it because of who he was and what he was that brought about the change? To catch a glimpse of the fullness of God with all of his great understanding of men and women, their passions and desires, their successes and failures, their joys and sorrows, their loves and hates.

To have the mind of Christ . . .

At this point negative questions almost overwhelm us. Did the promoter who thought up nefarious schemes to swindle hardworking people out of their life savings have the mind of Christ? What about the ones who perpetuate wars for gain? What about the ones who lurk in the shadows to mug and rob? Do those persons have the mind of Christ?

The answer must of necessity be yes, for the possibilities are there, but somehow, somewhere, the picture became distorted. This is the second step—to move from the negative to the positive.

At one time Jesus said, "For from his heart [mind] come the evil ideas which lead him to kill, commit adultery, and do other immoral things; to rob, lie, and slander others" (Matt. 15:19).

Today's scientists are telling us that the mind can be the beginning of every form of sin, disease, poverty, limitation, ignorance, and suffering just as it can be the substance of prosperity, health, happiness, wholeness. More and more we are coming to discover that the mind-set we have

THE ONE YOU CAN BECOME

determines to a great extent the way in which our lives are and will be shaped.

In *A Place to Stand,* Dr. Elton Trueblood wrote:

> Shocking as it sounds it is really possible for a finite man, as he responds to Christ's call, to have a measure of the spirit of Christ. The central purpose of the gospel is that Christ's nature may be formed in us (Gal. 4:19) and that he may dwell in our hearts. (Eph. 3:17)

The final step is to picture a magnet. It attracts certain substances, others it repels. So it is with our minds. We are either drawing people to us or we are repelling them. We can either attract health, happiness, and wholeness into our lives, or we can attract sickness, suffering, sorrow, and poverty. If we are in school, our thoughts will determine whether we stand at the top or the bottom of the class. A boy, who for years was satisfied if there were one other below him, suddenly became a leader in his field. A woman, who was afraid to make even the smallest report in her club, became a nationally recognized speaker at middle age.

If we start a business enterprise or choose a profession, our thoughts determine the extent to which it will succeed or fail.

To enter into marriage with the thought that it is a lifelong commitment, and that we will look for the best rather than the worst, is to insure the success of the union, but if we enter it with the thought that with the first disappointment it can be dissolved, then failure is merely a matter of time.

Here I would plead guilty to taking a sentence out of context, and yet it seems to have so many applications at this point that I cannot resist the temptation. It is where our Lord said, "I have opened a door in front of you, which no one can close" (Rev. 3:8). What is the door that he has opened for us? Isn't it the door of possibility—the possibility of faith, of achievement, of service without limit?

When God wants to bring about change he doesn't look

THE COMMAND POST

for method or organization, he looks for a man or a woman, one who is open to the possibilities that God has in mind. "God sent his messenger, a man named John, who came to tell people about the light" (John 1:6-7). "God gave the Law through Moses; but grace and truth came through Jesus Christ" (v. 17).

True mind, and here we must place emphasis on the word "true," has only one source, God, the creator and sustainer of the universe. Our mind is the mind of God working in and through us. True mind has only one thought: good for all creation. All evil thought patterns are a cancer that we have nurtured and allowed to run wild. Thoughts are but seeds that we have the power to cultivate or destroy. The power of choice is the great freedom that God, in his infinite goodness, has given to us as individuals. We can think in terms of the world—imperfection—or we can think in terms of the Spirit—perfection. To think only in terms of the physical is death. To think in terms of the Spirit is eternal.

We remember that Joshua said to his people, "Choose this day whom you will serve . . . but as for me and my house, we will serve the Lord." (Joshua 24:15 RSV).

Choice! What a wonderful gift! What an awesome responsibility!

When we make any choice, our mind becomes the command post to which our physical body responds.

Perhaps this is a good time to reflect on our past thinking. Which path have we chosen for our thoughts to follow? Have we indulged ourselves with pointless daydreaming, imagining that without any effort on our part some fairy godmother would touch us with a magic wand and give us something for nothing? Such dreams are useless because they lack concentration on our possibilities, which, when coupled with true faith, become realities. It is when we are working hand in hand with the indwelling Christ who is guiding us, strengthing us, encouraging us, the One who is

THE ONE YOU CAN BECOME

never defeated, that we climb the dizzying heights of all good.

Actually this is where we label ourselves. Rather than allowing our attention to dwell on the evil that so often surrounds us, we begin by placing a label upon ourselves that tells us exactly who we are—the children of God with the mind of Christ. We look long and carefully at this label that says we are 100 percent. We are neither damaged goods nor a blend. We are the genuine article created and sustained by God. To know this is to know exactly who we are and to know how to respond to every situation with which we are confronted. In our mind we fashion the perfect label and live up to it with all of our being, remembering that the one great power in the world and in our lives is God who is all good.

By so doing we honor the mind of Christ that is within us and give it free rein. By looking for and expecting the best, in fact by accepting nothing less than the best from ourselves at all times, we make welcome the Spirit of Christ who has always been waiting for our recognition.

With this thought uppermost we begin to realize what a marvelous creation we are. Actually in all of the billions of people who have walked the earth, or who will walk the earth, there will never be another just like us. For this reason we never try to imitate another or to be someone or something we are not. We are God's chosen personality with a definite plan and purpose.

We examine carefully the physical body that God has given us and discover that the best scientific mind has not yet invented a pump that will function as efficiently as our heart without an outside supply of power except that Universal Power. Nor has man invented a substance that will automatically renew itself year after year as do the cells of our bodies.

True, God has given some forms of animal life great bodies. He has given some plant forms a longer earthly life

THE COMMAND POST

span than ours, but because we have the power to think and have been given the freedom of choice, we have been given dominion over every plant and animal that inhabits the earth. When we were created, it was in the image of God; we were endowed with a portion of his mind. This, then, is why we can be confident of the judgments we are called upon to make if we first refer all decisions to him. We do not need to make this referral by formal request. We simply become still and realize the heritage that is ours. Because of this tremendous priceless resource we are enabled to make the right choices for the direction of our lives, be they as large as the choice of a career or a mate, or as simple as the necktie we will wear tomorrow.

When a thought of defeat or discouragement comes, we immediately replace it with the thought that such emotions have no place in the mind of Christ. If temptation comes we reject it as quickly as it appears, knowing that the Christ within would say that such things have no place in our lives with him.

True, at times we may expect too much. Again we do not expect enough. If, for example, we are expecting to see a complete change in ourselves immediately because we are changing our thought pattern, then we are expecting too much. On the other hand, if we do not see ourselves as eventually being totally renewed for the better with wholeness being our lot, then we are not expecting enough.

Slowly, day by day and night by night, we change. It, perhaps, is the nights that really work wonders. Even while we sleep, our thoughts penetrate our entire being, for there is one part of our mind that never sleeps—the subconscious. Consequently it is a good practice to program our nighttime mind with the positive before sleep comes. We do that by thanking God for the good mind he has given us and by asking him to help us to use it in the way he would have it used.

To do this is to lay a firm foundation for the coming day

THE ONE YOU CAN BECOME

when we move through the activities that demand so much of our attention until at best we only have brief intervals when we can think our own deeper thoughts; yet gradually we will begin to sense that these seed thoughts sown before going to sleep have taken root in our subconscious mind and given us direction in the most wonderful way.

Positive prayer is always a creative approach to life, and by using it faithfully and constructively it opens the way for a better life than that which we are presently enjoying. Thus, to end our active day with a thankful, yet expectant attitude is to be assured that on the morrow we will have the correct answers for questions that otherwise would be most perplexing. Again and again we would stress the fact that prayer is not limited to a religious activity. It is an essential approach to all positive activities of life. To integrate this into our lives, and to make it a part of all of our lives, we must stay with it until it becomes as natural as breathing.

Daily, even hourly, we affirm: "I am alive with the life of God. His life is my life."

To know that God is, and to be aware of the evidence around us, is the greatest assurance anyone can have. In times of doubt to open one's eyes and exclaim, "God is!" becomes the cornerstone for needed confidence and the courage to move in the right direction.

TO WORK MIRACLES

William Law, the eighteenth-century English clergyman, wrote: "If anyone would tell you the shortest, surest way to all happiness, and all perfection, he must tell you to make a rule for yourself, to thank and praise God that whatever seeming calamity happens to you, if you thank and praise God for it, you turn it into a blessing. Could you therefore work miracles, you could not do more for yourself than by this thankful spirit; for it heals with a word speaking, and turns all that it touches into happiness."

Helen Keller echoes this belief: "I thank God for my handicaps, for through them I have found myself, my work, and my God."

The psalmist wrote: "This is the day which the Lord has made; let us rejoice and be glad in it" (Ps. 118:24 RSV).

I was working at my desk when the telephone rang. Immediately I recognized the voice. He said, "I am absolutely at the end of my rope."

I heard the sharp intake of his breath when I said, "I am sure that you are." Before he could respond I asked, "Did you get any sleep last night?"

"Almost none," he replied. "Even the medicine didn't stop the pain. I can't stand it much longer."

It wasn't difficult to picture him. For years he had suffered so much, and now a recent accident when he had fallen and crushed his elbow, was added misery. At that very moment

THE ONE YOU CAN BECOME

I knew he had enough powerful medicine in his possession to end it long before I, or anyone else, could reach him.

In a play for time I said, "Across the years you have suffered so much, and you have a job that is very demanding. It takes everything you have."

He said, "Yes."

I asked. "Have you ever been in more pain than you are now?"

He hesitated. "I suppose once or twice," he said finally.

"Yet you made it," I said encouragingly.

"Yes," he replied, "with the help of the Lord. But right now I don't know what I believe. I know I can't pray any more. It doesn't seem to do any good."

There was a long pause. I called his name. At last he asked, "Will you pray for me?"

"Of course," I replied. "I have been praying for you."

"But I mean right now."

"Over the telephone?" I asked.

"Yes," he said, "over the telephone."

I said, "To begin I am going to thank God for hearing our prayer and responding to it. Will you pray along with me?"

"Yes," he said. And so we began our prayer together on a note of thanksgiving.

Later on in the day I called him. "How are you doing?" I asked. "I'm still in terrible pain," he replied, but I'm not as depressed as I was."

I said, "Then God heard our prayer and is responding to it."

"I hope so. I surely hope so."

"Of course he is," I said. Right at this moment God is in every fiber of your body, healing, strengthening, restoring. I want you to affirm that every few minutes.

"I'll try."

For many days I talked with him. His pain was so great; his discouragement so deep, and yet bit by bit he continued to struggle to surmount his problems just as he had done so many times before. Whenever I talk with him I think of Job who said, "Though he slay me, yet will I trust him" (Job 13:15 KJV).

When we are in an extreme situation physically or mentally this is the time to thank God with all of our heart until something changes either within ourselves or in the outer realm to give us direction.

It is not so much that we are thanking God for the pain, the confusion, the anxiety we are experiencing, as it is that we are thankful that he is with us and that he understands and is constantly working to bring things into harmony and restore us to our own good. If we are facing a seemingly dead-end street, this is the moment to thank God for all of the experiences we are having and to remember other situations when we thought we were at the end of our rope, but bit by bit new doors were opened. We remember that all the strength and courage we needed were given to us, and there was a way we could not miss.

A woman with two small children to support whose husband was dying of cancer so desperately needed a job. There was none. Still she never lost courage. Her faith never wavered. Then, one day she was given the opportunity to go back to college and finish her degree, making it possible for her to become a teacher, an ambition she had shunted aside when she married and became a mother. At first there seemingly had been no funds available, but suddenly there was a scholarship that had not been claimed, and she was able to borrow more money from the student loan fund. True, her husband did die, a tremendous loss to that little family, but she stood firm. Not only did she get her bachelor's degree, but she went on to get graduate degrees. She became nationally known in the education field. Her two children obtained college educations and advanced degrees. Then she found added happiness with another good husband.

Our first thought each morning upon awakening should

THE ONE YOU CAN BECOME

be one of thanksgiving for another opportunity to meet life head-on regardless of the prospects we are facing. Each day is another opportunity to marvel at the love and provision God has given us. Each new day is his special gift to us. Throughout the day we will encounter problems, perhaps some discouragement, but with every breath we are taking we are being filled with his life and his spirit. We literally take God into our being. Whether we recognize it or not, this is a fact we cannot escape. And with every heartbeat God is sending his life clear to our very fingertips.

Just as there may be some disappointments along the way, there will also be unexpected blessings if we keep ourselves open to them, expect them, and receive them as such. There is an ancient Indian poem that ends: "I am forever grateful for this beautiful and bountiful earth." And so we open our eyes to the beauty with which God has surrounded us.

I so well remember a time when for me everything had seemingly gone wrong. The work in which I was then engaged was not for me. I had made a terrible mistake in accepting it, or so I thought at the time. Later it was to become a tremendous asset, but then it was sheer drudgery. My responsibilities taxed my abilities to the utmost plus the fact that there was a sharp personality clash between my immediate superior and myself. Yet for a time I was locked into the situation, and I had not yet learned how to deal with such matters. That experience, like so many, was not to come until years later.

There came a noon when I was too miserable and discouraged to eat. As I walked along a busy street I passed an old gray stone church with ivy-covered walls when suddenly I saw a mother robin carrying a worm to her babies in a nest well concealed in the ivy. I paused to watch her. She seemed completely undisturbed by the roar of traffic. Her very manner seemed to say, "There is one who knows when even a sparrow falls." I thanked God for the

TO WORK MIRACLES

trust that mother bird exhibited as she lived up to her responsibilities, and so I would try to live up to mine until another door opened, which it eventually did, but not until I had learned some valuable lessons.

Every sunrise, every sunset, every bird that builds a nest, every flower that blooms, give testimony to the fact that God is working out his eternal purpose in spite of the convulsions of humanity if we will but thank him and give him the opportunity to fulfill his purpose for us.

It is not too difficult to be thankful when life is as tranquil as a wilderness lake at sunrise, but how does one honestly and sincerely express thanks when life has caved in? A terminal illness has been diagnosed. A mate, on whom one has depended so many years, suddenly is proven faithless. A lifetime of work has gone into a business enterprise and overnight it is wiped away. How can one be thankful under such circumstances?

Perhaps no one has suffered more than the apostle Paul, and he seems to have found the answer, for he wrote: "May you always be joyful in your union with the Lord." (Phil. 4:4).

Be joyful in your life in the Lord! True faith is joy regardless of the outer circumstances, joy because of our own deep inner life, secure with God. We begin by rejoicing or giving thanks that the one great power for all good is God, the creator and sustainer of life. We think back over all the good we have experienced in the past and are thankful for that. We are thankful that even in our time of testing, the love and power of God is at work in our lives. We rejoice that the Spirit of Christ is guiding us in our day-to-day decisions and meeting adequately all of our needs for the moment.

Even more we are filled with gratitude when we realize that no matter what the outer circumstances, the very presence of God is with us and that we cannot be separated from it unless we deliberately reject it.

The psalmist said, "Even though I walk through the valley of the shadow of death, I fear no evil; for thou art with me"

THE ONE YOU CAN BECOME

(Ps. 23:4 RSV). He also referred to the fact that God is "a very present help in trouble" (46:1 RSV).

Perhaps this is our great reason for thanksgiving; we are never alone. Illness, bereavement, economic disaster, do not separate us from the love of God.

The psalmist had discovered this. Paul likewise had made the great discovery, but how do we make such a discovery? As Shakespeare said, "That is the question."

Perhaps the first thing we need to do is to cease our frantic efforts and questioning to become still and know that God is God. For whether we realize it or not, our greatest suffering comes when God fades from our vision or his image becomes distorted. To lose sight of our God who is nearer than hands and feet, a God who is not only able but willing, in fact anxious, that we have life at its best is to stand alone, naked, in the storm of life.

Second, we thank him for being present with us and for understanding our problem whatever it may be. Not only do we thank him, but we affirm over and over again, "God understands. He is not confused. We will await with patience his answer."

Third, if the problem is in any way of our own making, we ask for his forgiveness and for the courage to make whatever restitution is necessary. As long as there remains anything that is not forgiven, we will never have the peace for which we so desperately long.

Finally, we release it all to him. If we need health, a job, money to pay bills, protection for self or for a loved one, we know that God is the Source of sources. All other means are only secondary, the channels through which he may or may not choose to work. We tell him that we are ready and willing to do our part when he shows us the way, and then with the perfect trust of a little child, we place it in his hands for safe keeping. With that we thank him that we can have perfect confidence in him for the solution, and immediately get busy with other matters.

TO WORK MIRACLES

When Elijah came to the end of his rope he was commanded to do certain things: he needed sleep and food to restore himself physically. After that he was given a task to perform. Elijah had complete faith, and he allowed God to direct his life (I Kings 19). Perhaps we can learn a great lesson from Elijah.

OUR HERITAGE

To say "our Father" is to claim our priceless heritage, but at the same time it calls for us to accept responsibility for all of life.

In the first two words of the model prayer, Jesus gave us the right to call ourselves children of God. This is the greatest privilege anyone can ever have, a child of the Most High, the Absolute Supreme, but with the privilege comes responsibility, the responsibility to handle wisely our legacy.

In theory it sounds so easy, but in actual practice it is a far different matter.

Take Donna; she is a classic example. When she came to a group seminar she said, "I don't know who I am." It was more than an admission, it was a desperate cry for help.

Several tried to help her, but for the most part what she was hearing were words, words without meaning. At the conclusion of the discussion she was no better off than she had been when she came.

Later a friend explained a little bit of Donna's problem. Apparently as a girl she had always been withdrawn and had experienced periods of desperate loneliness when she would spend long hours confiding to her dog. Even through college she continued to be a loner. Then one day she met a young army officer. He was not a career man but was anxious to return to his place in the business world. In terms of the old romantic novel he fell head over heels in love with this beautiful blonde whose quietness appealed to him. To protect her did something for his masculinity. In a matter of weeks they were married.

With his service completed they returned to his home city in an entirely different part of the country from her home. Because of her reticence she made few friends. In desperation she took a position for which she was not fitted. That only added to her confusion. To make matters worse, her husband, who had an outgoing personality, failed completely to understand her. He made the decisions while she meekly accepted them outwardly, but inwardly was crushed.

By the time Donna came to the seminar they were divorced. He wanted a woman who could keep pace with him, not one who was a drag, he told Donna in a fit of anger when she continued to shrink back. At this juncture she returned to her hometown, but by then the few friends she had known were either gone to other localities or had developed absorbing interests in jobs or families.

Again Donna found a job, this time as a salesperson in a department store where she was miserably unhappy. She had a small apartment where she spent her nights and weekends alone, eating her heart out because of her apparent failures in everything she had attempted.

It was sometime after the seminar when she was eating a solitary lunch in a restaurant that the woman who had taken her to the seminar came in and sat with her. In a burst of confidence Donna unburdened herself and concluded with the same cry, "If I only knew who I am! Somehow I've got to find myself."

The friend listened. "Don't you really know who you are?" she asked.

Donna shook her head. "No. Not the way other people do, not the way you do. You are a success. I am a failure."

There were many such luncheons together. Little by little Donna revealed herself to her friend. After some months

THE ONE YOU CAN BECOME

she was included in a group that met weekly for study and sharing.

One evening as Donna and her friend were driving home from one of their group meetings she blurted out as if she did not realize quite what she was saying, "Now I know. I really know who I am. I'm just what you have been trying to tell me. I'm a child of God. Do you realize what that means to me?"

Her's was a slow process, for society had already left its mark on her, but bit by bit as her newfound confidence increased, her sales record improved so much that her supervisor noticed her. There were two promotions in rapid succession.

Then one evening in a group session Donna startled those present as well as herself, no doubt, when she said, "You know the reason my sales record improved. I kept thinking about the prayer I had been praying. It wasn't 'my Father'; it was 'our Father.' Suddenly I saw my customers in a new light. Our Father is all inclusive. They were children of God just as I was. It made all the difference in the world. I didn't see them as someone to fear. I saw them as persons God loved. Ours was a spiritual kinship. I listened to them in a different way, and I was able to talk with them."

Later, in telling about this, Donna's friend, Madeline, said, "I think we finally related to one another because I too had once felt rejected. A person such as Donna cannot be reached through intellectual theory, which at best only touches the outside. It is not until one is touched inwardly because he or she knows that another has lived through a similar expeience and has found help that changes occur. At the seminar when we talked about being a child of God, it was meaningless babble to her, but as we shared, something came through to her. As a result I too am strengthened in my faith. I really feel like a child of God."

After a pause she added, "The loneliness, the sense of

OUR HERITAGE

failure that gnawed at her, were not just her problems alone. They became problems of all of us who pray, "our Father."

It was the prophet who asked, "Have we not all one father? Has not one God created us? Why then are we faithless to one another?" (Mal. 2:10 RSV).

The Judeo-Christian tradition stands squarely on the fact that all men are brothers, and it implies that in the strictest sense we cannot rise to a better life unless we help others improve their lot.

In this fashion, Mahatma Gandhi, who had once been shunned by those of a different race, declared, "I am a Mohammedan and a Hindu, a Christian and a Jew."

Theologically we might disagree, but in the realm of the Spirit he was correct, for we are all of those if we subscribe to the belief that we have a common father, God. This immediately cuts away the idea of a superior race, even a superior person.

"Superior to what?" we ask. Because of our environment, our educational advantage, the various opportunities some of us have had, we may have advanced in some areas of life more than others, but to come back to the basics of the Spirit, or what we are in the sight of God, the thoughts of such a thing as complete superiority vanish. In the words of the Son, "We are one in the Spirit."

Here we break through the realm of history and time and move into that of eternity, limitlessness, and timelessness. In no way are any of us creatures set apart from God, against God, or against one another. Rather we are all endowed with a divine nature, and have been since the beginning of time, and as such are participants in a divine plan that began with creation.

It then follows that if we are children of God, we are to accept the responsibility of our legacy and become conscious of the oneness of everyone, even everything.

The Hindu philospher says, "There is nothing in the universe that is not God, everlasting Spirit. Everything lives in Spirit; it is the seed of all seeds, from it everything comes."

In the light of these words we remember, "All things were made through him, and without him was not anything made that was made" (John 1:3 RSV).

A geologist holding a rock said, "Even this isn't dead as we once believed. It is involved in a constant motion of energy. The crystals of which it is composed are moving, each one a world in itself."

Pierre Teilhard de Chardin, one of the great contemporary thinkers and writers has written, "As a man awakens to a sense of universal unification, everything glows as if impregnated with the essential flavor of the absolute beyond all ideologies and systems to a different and higher sphere, a new spiritual dimension."

To fully consider the all inclusiveness of the two words "our Father" is not only to see our divine heritage but to see God in everything and, because of our divine nature, our ownership in everything and our responsibility for everything. Thus we find ourselves in tune with a dynamic force. It is a thought that will require all of eternity if we are to fully comprehend its magnitude, but in a moment it can start us on a journey of unlimited adventure.

A DIVINE PLAN

There are those who see religion as a copout, a trick whereby we refuse to accept any responsibility of our own by saying that everything is, or isn't, God's will. Not so. If we accept the fact that God is our Father, it stands to reason that he would have a plan for us, but rather than relieving us of responsibility it could entail more responsibility on our part, the responsibility of ascertaining what he wants us to do with our lives, our abilities, in the time we have left whether we are eighteen or eighty and then moving steadily ahead.

We look back to the experience of Donna and Madeline cited in the previous chapter. Some would say that Donna just happened to be in the right place, which was a restaurant, at the right time, or when Madeline entered. Those persons try to explain such happenings by talking in terms of luck, happenstance, chance.

Again I would feel compelled to say, "not so," for as I look back on a rather full life and as I view it as a whole, there are so many things that dovetail together, there is no doubt in my mind that these were all a part of a plan. The times of failure, of disappointment, most generally came as a result of plunging ahead, taking things in my own hands with my eyes fixed on the immediate rather than the overall scheme of things. When one looks to God for direction coincidences do happen.

In the case of Donna and Madeline, both had abilities,

both had responsibilities. Donna had the ability to become an outstanding salesperson once she was able to overcome her feeling of reticence. Madeline had the responsibility of befriending, understanding, even extending a helping hand, and as a result both lives were benefited.

How many times we say, "I didn't know which way to turn, then an idea came to me."

In a delightful little book, *It Came to Me,* written by Harry V. Richardson, president emeritus of Interdenominational Theological Center in Atlanta, Georgia, the author recounts the story of a wife of a sharecropper in Alabama. In the book the woman tells that they were so terribly poor, then at the age of sixty-three, after failing again and again she looked at the pitiful little three-room shack they called home and was ready to cry. She said, "All at once it came to me that I didn't need to be poor like that. It just came to me that the same God who made other people made me. The same God who loved other people loved me. The same God who helped other people would help me if I would try to be what I ought to be." Then she tells how idea after idea just seemed to come to her for improving their lot; but once she had the idea she didn't just sit idly by and wait for things to happen. She got busy and made them happen.

So it was with Donna. Once she realized the meaning of the words "our Father" she had prayed, she made things happen by listening and talking with her customers.

While we believe that God has a divine plan for everyone, we do not believe that he attempts to dictate. His plan is that we lead a purposeful, productive life filled with joyful interests, health, and prosperity. In no way is God a selfish parent who tries to fulfill his own ambitions by forcing a child in a direction contrary to his or her best abilities.

A man who has given his life to athletics, and who at one time was named coach of the year by his state high school athletic association, has only one son who is not interested in sports as an active participant. He is an outstanding

A DIVINE PLAN

young pianist with the help and encouragement of his father, who is as proud of his accomplishments in the concert hall as he would be had the boy been a star quarterback. The father has only one desire, and that is to see his son develop and make full use of his God-given talents.

Some catechisms tell us that our "chief aim is to glorify God." While this is the way in which we find true happiness, to glorify or express the essential nature or purpose of God it must be emphasized that this does not mean in a religious sense only. The one who paints a beautiful picture, builds a labor-saving device, teaches a child, keeps a highway open, serves in any way to make life better, is glorifying God. Jesus said even to give a cup of cold water in his spirit was to magnify him.

Thus we too have a part in bringing a divine plan into the world. We pray for direction that by our actions we may have a part in the fulfillment of this plan. If there is to be divine order in the world we must accept gladly our responsibility. We keep ourselves in harmony with God and develop a right relationship with others. We know that such a plan is always accompanied by love and understanding and that it looks for good in everyone, in every situation.

If there is a lack of harmony in the home, the school, the marketplace, we work to restore peace and wholeness by knowing that trouble and unhappiness are not a part of God's plan but are caused by persons not living up to their best. We know that God's harmony is able to overcome human inharmony, therefore we hold fast to that which is good until the divine plan is once more established.

Prayer, meditation, and the Bible help us to become receptive to God's plan for us. There is no better place to begin than with the Bible. It is the greatest guidebook ever written, for it is a book that deals so much with our attitudes toward self and others.

For the one looking for direction the prophet Micah in his

THE ONE YOU CAN BECOME

definition of true religion capsules it so poignantly for us. "He has showed you, O man, what is good; and what does the Lord require of you but to do justice, and to love kindness, and to walk humbly with your God?" (Mic. 6:8 RSV).

To incorporate those suggestions into one's life-style would bring about such drastic changes that literally the average person would not recognize himself or herself.

For the one who faces life with the feeling of insecurity, loneliness, to take to heart the words found in the writings of another ancient prophet, "Fear not, for I am with you. . . . I will strengthen you, I will help you, I will hold you with my victorious right hand" (Isa. 41:10 RSV), will have the assurance that God is right there, comforting, strengthening, sustaining as any concerned father. In effect he is saying, "My child, take courage. I am right here with you."

When our thoughts are centered in God, we no longer are burdened with our own mistaken ideas of self. In quietness and confidence we open ourselves to the free flow of the mind of God. As we trust him for the right answers to our anxieties, the wonder-working power of infinite intelligence directs us into ways that we perhaps would never have dreamed possible had we continued in our own way.

While writing this chapter I took time out for lunch with a young man and his wife. The man, still in his early thirties, is moving up rapidly in his chosen profession—engineering. His responsibilities are heavy. Fifteen years ago he seemed headed for failure, then through a series of coincidences (he had a devoted, praying mother) things began to happen.

During the luncheon he said, "To have an effective prayer life translated into terms of daily living calls for our acceptance and living of two factors—faith and obedience. If we have faith in God as exemplified by Jesus Christ, and obey the direction of the inner voice we can move mountains."

A DIVINE PLAN

When we, as individuals, came into being, God already had a divine plan built into our very souls. It was there just as much as the plan for a great oak is wrapped up in the shell of a tiny acorn.

How wonderful it would be if parents and teachers, who have the responsibility for children in their formative years, could sense this. So much confusion and uncertainty could be avoided.

Because a boy had difficulty with grammar, a teacher said, "Perhaps you should think more along the line of manual arts." Later, in college, a teacher said, "You have the ability to express yourself. I'd like to help you become a writer." Because the thought of manual arts had been so firmly implanted in that young mind, it was years before the transition was made. Eventually that one became a newspaper reporter, a magazine writer, and finally the author of several books. I know because I was that boy.

A man, almost at retirement age who had tried many jobs, none too successfully, said, "I have never been able to find myself." When asked what he would have been if he had his life to live over again he replied, "I would have been an archeologist, but when I mentioned it to my father he said if I just wanted to dig in the dirt why didn't I become a gravedigger so I gave up the idea."

Today there are so many who do not know what they want to do with their lives. If they would only pause in their frantic search to find self and look to the One who breathed the very breath of life into their being they would find that a specific plan would unfold naturally.

A young man finishing a state university in the upper 10 percent of his class confided, "In this day of materialism money must be the prime consideration. I don't want to be pigeonholed. I want to be where I can move and move fast."

When asked what other requirements he had fixed for himself as he is applying for a position he said. "Naturally I

THE ONE YOU CAN BECOME

would want to like my work and those with whom I work if possible. After that I guess it doesn't much matter."

Never should we think of a divine plan as being a selfish plan, one that will benefit only the individual. Any plan the Creator had in mind for us is not limited to the individual alone but would invariably reach out and touch the lives of many, bringing harmony and prosperity with almost unlimited outreach.

To know that in the divine plan we are only asking for that which is our perfect right to have and to make it manifest is to think on a larger scale than self alone. If releases from our minds doubt, fear, jealously, and greed. It affords the courage and the initiative to do those things that are ours to do. We no longer ask why some have certain abilities and we do not. We are not envious. Rather we are free to proceed with the utmost expectation, and because we have a joyful expectation we also have the necessary enthusiasm that brings our desires to fulfillment. In fact the prerequisite for becoming a receiver is to become a giver.

Once more we think of Donna and Madeline. Madeline gave of herself. In so doing she realized that she had abilities she never before had realized, the ability to reach out and touch another life. Up until that time she had never thought of herself as working in a personnel department. As she saw Donna making progress she realized that others might also be in need of understanding and acceptance. It opened a new door for her. While she was not in a position to quit her job and go back to school full time she took a few evening classes. A few months later there was an opening in the company for which she worked for one with her qualifications. She applied for it and was accepted.

If we truly believe there is a divine plan for us, perhaps the initial step is to become givers, not of material things only, but givers of understanding, forgiveness, a helping hand, and best of all the gift of self back to God so that he may work his perfect will in us and through us, thus bringing his

A DIVINE PLAN

divine plan for us into harmony with his plan for all of creation.

In conjunction with this, we begin by thanking God that a divine plan is already at work in our lives. We are assured that his Spirit fills our being during the busy hours of the day and in the dark of night. We thank him that a divine plan is our inheritance and that nothing can separate us from his love.

Finally, when faced with a decision we thank him that we can turn to him, knowing that he has the perfect plan already mapped out for us. When difficulties arise, and they will from time to time, we relase them to him knowing that he will cooperate with us to set them aright. Because we trust him for the perfect plan by committing our desires to him, we erase all negative thoughts and find ourselves restored to peace of mind, a priceless possession. We affirm that we are living souls put here for a purpose, and that purpose is to grow and to be a credit to our creator, ourselves and our fellowmen.

In *Learning to Grow Old,* Paul Tournier, a Swiss psychologist, medical doctor, and author, has written:

I believe that God has a plan for every man at every moment. This conviction can give a new dimension to the reflection to which I was calling retired persons just now. There is no more fertile source for the creative imagination than prayer and meditation.

GOOD JUDGMENT

It was one of those situations that literally explode without warning. The meeting of key staff personnel of a large corporation had been called to formulate plans for the coming year. Before the meeting was an hour old, one of the junior members of the group demanded and was given the right to speak. His voice was angry. His statements were jampacked with emotion. Charges, particularly against the management, were made. The word "discrimination" was repeated. Finally the speaker, perspiring and exhausted, sat down.

Other members of the group looked anxiously to the manager of the corporation toward whom most of the charges had been made. For a few moments he sat quietly with no trace of emotion in his manner. Finally he stood up. "I've been listening to what my young friend had to say. He made a number of suggestions we need to consider. I am glad that he felt free enough to bring his problems to us for solution. I believe there are answers just as I believe that as we work together in harmony we will have a successful year."

Later, when asked by one of his colleagues how he managed to keep his cool, he smiled, "You didn't need to ask that. You know the motto I keep on my desk. I try to live by it." The motto to which he referred was, "In quietness and in trust shall be your strength" (Isa. 30:15 RSV).

An executive in another corporation told a group of men

GOOD JUDGMENT

that many times when he is facing a decision he leaves his desk, goes to a park nearby, and there he seeks God to help him clear his mind of the clutter and confusion he is experiencing and to make the decision that will be most beneficial to all concerned.

Many have found great help by referring to The Four-Way Test. (1) Is it the truth? (2) Is it fair to all concerned? (3) Will it build goodwill and better friendships? (4) Will it be beneficial to all concerned?

The president of another large corporation wrote that his company achieved outstanding success by adhering to those principles in all of their considerations.

The late Samuel Shoemaker said there are four absolutes in the Sermon on the Mount: absolute honesty, absolute purity, absolute unselfishness, and absolute love.

It is important to remind ourselves again and again of the down-to-earth teaching of the Christian faith. It is a practical philosophy of life that one can make his or her own and that in faith and obedience we live. Where can one find greater help than from the Proverbs concerned primarily with the common problems of living? Some of these concerns deal with family relations or our business involvement with others. Some are concerned with matters of etiquette in social relationships, others with the need for self-control. Definitely they have much to say about such qualities as humility, patience, respect for the poor, and loyalty to friends.

When we pray for sound judgment we can begin by thanking God that he has seen fit to give us such a wonderful guidebook and that we are thankful for his indwelling presence to guide and direct us. Our prayers for guidance do not need to be either long or complicated. In *Contemplative Prayer,* the late Thomas Merton quotes a monk from the Desert Fathers who asked St. Macarius how to pray. The latter replied: "It is not necessary to use many words. Only stretch out your arms and say: 'Lord, have pity

THE ONE YOU CAN BECOME

on me as you desire, and as you well know how!' And if the enemy presses you hard, say: 'Lord, come to my aid!' "

To face facts squarely there are many times when we are hesitant to ask our Lord for direction because it may commit us to a way of life we do not honestly desire. Too often we seek the benefit of prayer; yet at the same time try to avoid total commitment and what it would entail. It is there that our self-love, our own selfish desires influence the response to our prayers. And because we are human it is not easy to preempt our minds of these influences.

Perhaps here our first concern should be to formulate a very careful picture of the person we would like to be, not only how we want the world to see us, but how we want to see ourselves and how we want God to see us. To formulate such a picture and to hold to it will determine well in advance the way in which we will make many of our decisions.

One definite question we might ask ourselves is, Will the way in which I make this decision in any way violate my own integrity? In other words, Can I live with it comfortably and face unashamedly all who may eventually know about it? Another question we might ask, If I know by this action it can change my life do I want it so changed?

One who had years of experience in making decisions said, "If you have been struggling with a problem all day and find yourself wavering, do not make the decision in the closing hours of the day, but sleep on it."

Twice the writer has been faced with the decision of a job change that involved moving to a different locality. Twice the decision was made to change. Both times, after sleeping on it and upon awakening in the morning there was a clear-cut decision to remain, and ensuing years have borne out the fact that the second decision was the correct one.

Why sleep on it? Simply because during the relaxed

GOOD JUDGMENT

hours of sleep the creative part of the mind, that part which has our own best interests at heart, is able to work without outside influences and rely completely on the indwelling presence of the divine mind.

This immediately brings up another question, "Are we willing to face the truth?"

A very intelligent young woman was engaged to be married. Her friends, her parents, and her pastor advised against it. While the man in question had a most delightful personality, one that could charm a cricket off the hearth, he was most unreliable plus the fact that he had an alcohol problem and had already failed in one marriage attempt. That girl refused to face the truth. She argued that there were those instances when marriage had changed a person completely, and she was correct in that assumption, but on a very small percentage basis. Later, she was to acknowledge that in her quieter moments she knew how slim the chances of success were, but before she was unwilling to admit that she might be making a mistake. Because of her inability to face the truth they were married, only to have the union end in a very painful divorce after she had been beaten unmercifully by her husband.

What about the lesser decisions? A businessman gives this advice, especially about purchases. Ask yourself, "Do I just want it, or do I really need it?" And in the case of a major purchase, wait three days before making the decision. With that in mind we might walk through our homes and look at the things we have bought and ask, "Would I really have purchased this had I waited three days?"

On a more personal nature, what about our thinking? Here we think of the proverb which might serve as a guideline. "For as he thinketh in his heart, so is he" (Prov. 23:7 KJV).

To repeat an earlier question, but with a different wording, If we knew that by harboring a thought there was a

THE ONE YOU CAN BECOME

possibility that it might change our lives would we want to continue with that thought? We may feel that we have little control over the exterior of our lives, but we do have control over our thoughts. While it is not always easy to change our thought pattern or to keep unbidden thoughts from popping up in our minds, we can change them step by step as we realize that such thinking has no place in the divine mind and by moving away from those outside influences that might stimulate thoughts that are less than our best.

Read any newspaper with this thought in mind, "If these persons had thought differently would this ever have happened?" It is a most revealing experience.

Certainly there are peer pressures. While this applies to all of us, it is especially true of the younger generation. A judge who has spent many years on the bench dealing largely with family and juvenile problems says no one knows the peer pressure placed upon our young people. The temptations in so many areas are untold times greater than young people experienced twenty-five or thirty years ago, he contends. He says that very often his heart breaks for them because under pressure they have made the wrong decision. Yet he says he can only say to them, "Why do you not judge for yourselves the right thing to do?" (Luke 12:57).

Then he says to them, "Why not bet on yourself? Often the difference between success and failure is the one who has the courage to decide for him or herself." He adds that we often think of great courage on the athletic field or during a crisis, but everyday living requires the courage of our convictions if we are to be successful.

Finally, for all of us there comes the element of risk. Try as we will we make mistakes, even fail, have to backtrack, still we must not let this deter us from working toward our goal, keeping intact the picture of the person we want to become with God's help.

Good judgment that comes from divine guidance can be

GOOD JUDGMENT

ours as we come to realize that God is with us at all times. Whenever we are willing to cooperate with the Holy Spirit—Christ's indwelling presence—our path will become increasingly clear. We think differently. We live differently when we realize that God is with us. We are never alone.

PROSPERITY

We were sitting around the fire on an island deep in the wilderness where we were camped for the night, talking long thoughts as men will at times like that, when the conversation drifted to the subject of prosperity.

After listening for several minutes, the guide asked, "Isn't prosperity relative? We are all interested in it, not just in theory, but money, health, resources, whatever it takes to get along. Back in the cities where you men live it may depend on the stock market, a sales report, good investments, belonging to the right club. Out here in the wilderness it's different. A few good lures to take fish, a warm sleeping bag, some essentials in the grub sack to supplement the fish we catch and the berries we pick. There isn't one of us tonight who has brought along a complete change of clothing, but I believe we are fairly content. I have seen so many who were a success on their jobs, but I question if they were a success in life."

I knew something about the one who had just spoken. Ten years before he had been in an executive position with an oil company. One day he resigned, and he and his wife returned to their native state in the north country where together they built a modest home with a garden. Both were licensed guides, meeting people, often talking to people just as he had talked with us.

The editor of a daily paper said, "I seem to remember a speech that a physician by the name of Sir William Osler once made. His thesis was that we need to learn to live in day-tight compartments. Give your best today and forget yesterday and tomorrow.

"Jesus said, 'Take no thought for the morrow.' In his teachings and life-style he detailed God's own blueprint for life. He definitely believed in prosperity even though his personal possessions consisted of a seamless robe. He taught it over and over again. 'I have come in order that you might have life—life in all its fullness' (John 10:10). That is prosperity. In his model prayer he said, 'Give us today the food we need' (Matt. 6:11). While it is true that Jesus was speaking of food, he was speaking of far more than any substance we may put in our mouths. He was speaking of all of our needs, spiritual as well as physical.

"Because Jesus' teachings were complete, he never spoke of a need or a goal without telling us how to achieve that end. He said, 'Be concerned above everything else with the Kingdom of God and with what he requires of you, and he will provide you with all these other things' (Matt. 6:33). This Kingdom that we are seeking is an inner kingdom, a kingdom made up of faith, love, joy, strength, understanding, enthusiasm, trust, and life itself. That's prosperity." He paused and poked at the fire. "I guess I've got an editorial for the Saturday afternoon paper when I go back to the shop."

The greatest prosperity one can have is peace of mind. Nevertheless, do not think one cannot have peace of mind and still have money. Very often those who do not have money think more about it than those who do, for they need it so badly for their daily necessities.

At the conclusion of a class I was teaching, a woman said, "I have so much: a beautiful home, good clothes, means to travel, a wonderful husband; does this bar me from the kingdom of heaven?"

Because I have known her over a long period of time I could respond with a quick no.

She gives her best to every task for which she has

THE ONE YOU CAN BECOME

responsibility. She gives unstintingly to her church. She is well organized, does not waste, gives all the credit for her success to God. Above all she is extremely generous with her possessions. She shares both her spiritual blessings and her material blessings with those who stand in need of either or both.

While money, as we usually think of it, is a very physical commodity, a medium of exchange, it can also become spiritual as it is used to bring God's kingdom into a living reality. Again how? (1) By remembering. "You shall remember the Lord your God, for it is he who gives you power to get wealth" (Deut. 8:18). (2) God is the prime source, all others are secondary, our jobs, our crops, our investments; these may fail but never God. To place our trust in God frees his mighty power within us. This God-given power can create, can produce, can sustain, can protect, can guide. (3) Not only do we look to the source, but we thank him that he is the source and that as such he is utterly dependable to meet our every need. To realize that he is the source eliminates worry and as a result leaves us free to act in the manner in which he would have us to act. It is the very Spirit of God within us that frees us from any thought of limitation. He is the source of infinite supply. As Jesus taught, it is when we live in a realization of our oneness with the Source of sources rather than with the thought of self only, that our needs will be met. This is the first law of prosperity, to look to God for all things.

Out of the limitless abundance of the universe there is sufficient to meet the needs (but not the greeds) of everyone. Whenever we think of prosperity we must differentiate between needs and greeds. As Thoreau said, "A man is rich in proportion to the number of things which he can afford to let alone."

Evelyn Underhill wrote:

We mostly spend our lives congugating three verbs: to Want, to Have, and to Do. Craving, clutching, and fussing on the material,

PROSPERITY

political, social, emotional, intellectual—even on the religious plane, we are kept in perpetual unrest; forgetting that none of these verbs has ultimate significance, except so far as they are transcended by and included in the fundamental verb, to Be; and that Being, not wanting, having and doing is the essence of a spiritual life.

Life, true life, is poetry when we give more importance to the inner spirit than we do to the outer shell. To be something is more important than to get something.

In his book *The Simple Life,* Vernard Eller says, "For Jesus, self-denial is more like a swimmer getting rid of his outer clothing in order to truly enjoy his swimming."

The second great law of prosperity is giving. Jesus said, "Give to others, and God will give to you. Indeed, you will receive a full measure, a generous helping, poured into your hands—all that you can hold. The measure you use for others is the one God will use for you" (Luke 6:38).

In conversation a man said, "This talk of giving is all right for those who have. They can afford to give and will not be hurt by it, but it has no place in the life of those who are poor."

That man had two mistaken ideas. He did not see that God is the Source of sources, and he had a mistaken idea of prosperity. He saw giving or prosperity purely in terms of material. In those terms, Jesus had so little to give; yet he gave so much. He gave understanding, forgiveness, health, love, a way of life to those who sought and accepted, and eventually he gave his life. There, even he discovered how difficult it is to share with those who do not understand because they do not really want to understand.

Imagine, if we can, sitting down in a crowd and listening to Jesus as he talked about giving and receiving, about putting God first in our lives and others second. Imagine what would happen in our relationships with others at work, in the home, if we gave love, faith, understanding, joy, and enthusiasm to them.

THE ONE YOU CAN BECOME

When we want more of anything we give more of self.

The renowned soprano, Janet Baker, has a sense of what she terms "holy obligation" regarding her spectacular voice which has thrilled thousands across the world. She says "My gift is God-given. . . . And it must be given back. . . . We all have a gift to give." If we find out what our gifts are and give them back with a sense of holy obligation, we will have valuable lives.

True, there are those who have tried giving for a time, namely in the material realm, and with their giving they have prayed for pay increases, healing, a happy marriage, understanding of children, and seemingly their prayers have not been answered. Here both the disbeliever and the skeptic fail to consider the two great threads that run all through our relationship with God—faith and obedience. Without being judgmental it is obvious that such persons have not honestly tried God's generosity by putting him first in their lives, by trusting him without reservation, and obeying him completely.

Never think that prosperity is a deal in which we give to God so that he will give to us. In the final analysis, it means giving our entire self to him to be directed by him. However, if we do put him first where the material is concerned, proving our trust by our actions and not just looking at it as a mere theory that we will try for a brief time, we will eventually put him first in everything we do.

To put our trust in God and prove it by giving ourself to him without reservation will bring about such a change in our lives that no force on earth can turn us from the happiness we receive. The only difference between those who succeed and those who fail is the pattern of their thoughts. Right thinking is the key to all success. Wrong thinking is a straight path to failure.

True prosperity is a habit that must be practiced and developed. We begin when we say "our Father," knowing

PROSPERITY

that he wants us to all have what we need from his limitless supply.

Nevertheless, with receiving comes responsibility. We have the responsibility to become good stewards of God's provision for us. To do this we must learn to give of our time, our talents, our best. Through sloppy work, not caring about our appearance, not honestly trying to use our God-given opportunities, we are not demonstrating that we are created in the spiritual image of God. We do not need more opportunity; rather we need the ability to see and grasp our opportunities. God's abundant gifts are all around if we but pause to look for them.

George Washington Carver discovered three hundred new uses for the lowly peanut and one hundred fifty new uses for the sweet potato. For all of that he did not receive a material fortune, although he was offered one, but he will live in history as one of the immortals who gave so much to all humankind and blazed a new path of hope for his race.

The writer, the scientist, the painter, are prospered by creative ideas. A doctor who stayed with a patient one night only to make him comfortable, in what were thought to be his final hours, suddenly had an idea. He tried it, and it proved successful. Later, when the patient tried to thank him he said, "Don't thank me, thank God. That idea came from him."

When the mind is centered on God, who supplies all positive ideas, that person is asking the one great mind to reveal all the necessary ideas for guidance and success. Never think, however, that such ideas are a result of mere daydreaming. Rather they come during those moments when we are trusting wholly in God. God does not keep any needed ideas from his children. He always does his part, but for success he expects us to take action and put his ideas to work.

A minister who gives untold hours to counseling says that he finds money to be the greatest cause of marital discord.

THE ONE YOU CAN BECOME

He says, "I tell those people who come to me to determine to live on 80 percent of their income, to save 10 percent, and to give 10 percent and quote to them the ancient prophet, 'Bring the full tithes into the storehouse, that there may be food in my house; and thereby put me to the test, says the Lord of hosts, if I will not open the windows of heaven for you and pour down for you an overflowing blessing' (Mal. 3:10 RSV). I tell them to look to God for guidance, to ask him to direct their giving, and that upon occasion it may be where they least expect to use it for him. For it is here that only the individual in cooperation with the Spirit within can make that decision."

Perhaps for too long we have filled our minds with fear, doubt, and skepticism until there is no room for receiving the blessings God wants to pour into our lives. Consequently we resolve to keep our minds filled with his great love, to look to him as the source, to give as he would have us to give and then to move out into the full stream of life with joyful expectancy.

We begin today to declare war on poverty in every area of life by cooperating with the One who creates abundance. To affirm wholeness by action is to do the things we know are right in the sight of God.

We believe that prosperity is part of God's divine plan for his children. His is a bountiful supply. We can never ask as much from him as he has given us or wants to continue to give us if we will but receive it. As E. Stanley Jones has written, "If God guides, God provides."

HEALING

To state that any disease, any condition, is incurable is to doubt the power of the living God. If the divine source of life can heal a cut finger, a bruised knee, is it not possible to suppose that this same source can heal the most stubborn malignancy? Divine healing and medical practice go hand in hand. They complement each other by bringing wholeness to the entire person. Nothing is incurable when trusted to God. God is able. At the same time medical science is making tremendous progress. We aid both God and science by holding a mental picture of perfect restoration in our minds until it is more than a picture, it becomes a reality. Encouragement builds, discouragement destroys.

Of all the miracles performed by Jesus, the greatest number had to do with healing. To heal the sick in body, mind, and soul is one of the basic commands of the healing Christ (Matt. 10:8).

Actual healing power has always belonged to God. Medicine does not heal. Doctors and surgeons do not heal. Therapy does not heal. Rest or climatic change do not heal. All healing is of God. However, he does continually use these various agents and many more to bring about healing.

Inscribed over the entrance to the College of Surgeons in Paris are these words: "I dressed the patient's wounds;

THE ONE YOU CAN BECOME

God healed him." At the entrance to the Columbia-Presbyterian Medical Center in New York City these words are for all to see: "For from the Most High cometh healing."

Because the physical and the spiritual are so closely intertwined, one with the other, healing must always be concerned with the total person. Many times the basic need is for physical healing. Again it may be there is need for mental or spiritual healing. Time after time Jesus talked of two things: forgiveness and action. "Your sins are forgiven. . . . Take up your bed. . . . Go wash. . . . Go show yourself."

Forgiveness, cleansing, freeing, by whatever name we may call it, we are asking to be relieved of something that is causing suffering. It may be a condition brought about as a result of our own actions or thinking. Again it may be something over which we have no control, but whatever it is, we are asking to be relieved of the illness that is troubling us, not just for our own sake, but that we may be truly useful in the kingdom of God here and now.

To begin with, true faith inspires healthy thinking, healthy living, right relationships with our universe. This is the best preventative of ill health we can have. If, by some stretch of imagination, an individual from his early life really lived with the thought that the body is the temple of the living God, much of our present-day sickness could be avoided. Unfortunately, too many of us do not assume this responsibility, perhaps because we have never been taught, or in our hurry we have ignored it.

Not only does true faith teach the proper care of the physical body, but it encourages honest work, which has a definite therapeutic value. True faith encourages rest and relaxation. It encourages meditation, prayer, worship, all of which have a therapeutic effect. To study the Bible is to find an antidote to fear, anxiety, and guilt. Over and over again Jesus stressed the necessity of forgiveness by replacing fear with the stronger emotion of love. Love is an emotion,

HEALING

but it is also a healing spiritual quality. Many, many persons have literally been loved back to health and wholeness.

Anger and hate attract disease by causing a lack of harmony in our entire physical and mental system. For many the greatest necessity is to look honestly at a problem and say, "I completely forgive." We are told in the Bible not to let the sun go down on our wrath. Medical science affirms that statement. Forgiveness, difficult though it may be, is not only possible but wonderfully healing. It unlocks whatever has stood between us and our own good.

Over and over again, doctors and psychologists tell us that their waiting rooms and hospital beds are crowded by persons who would not need to be there if they would only correct their thinking. Some have placed the figures as high as 75 percent. Our thoughts are either building us up or tearing us down. The body has no initiative of its own. It is completely at the mercy of the mind. We flush with anger, grow cold with fright, become excited with anticipation, lose our appetite when confronted with unpleasantness.

In this modern age of high-speed living, tension plays such a major role in many of our ills: hypertension, digestive disturbances, coronary problems. Doctors are now telling us that such common thing as dandruff is often caused by too much tension. A doctor who is greatly troubled by it while engaged with his practice has testified that when on vacation and away from pressures it entirely disappears.

Because tension is such a part of daily life for the majority of us, we cannot close our eyes to it. How do we live with it and maintain an emotional balance that does not rob us of health or leave us completely drained of energy we might devote to happier hours?

Perhaps more than anything we need to determine what our true goals in life are. There are those who have decided they will be satisfied with less of the material to be relieved of the stress and strain that comes with high-pressure living. How fortunate they are if they can achieve this life-style and

THE ONE YOU CAN BECOME

still meet adequately the demands of already acquired responsibilities, such as families for example.

But is there an answer for those who cannot escape? Perhaps one of the greatest releases is to pause, even momentarily, and realize the indwelling presence of the living Lord, knowing beyond a doubt that he is able to see us through any event that may arise. To know that one is not alone, but that there is a source of strength far greater than our own, can do much to calm taut nerves that are literally screaming for release. This is the time to quietly affirm, "I have an active, vital, miracle-working faith. I place my complete trust in God, knowing that he is able to bring blessings out of this situation now causing so much tension. While I work at the problem he is working in and through me toward a successful solution."

The second way to eliminate tension is to keep oneself in proper physical condition by rest, exercise, and the elimination of habits that might contribute to the problem.

Finally, a third way to eliminate tension is to live in day-tight compartments, that is, to deal with one problem at a time. Jesus said, "So do not worry about tomorrow; it will have enough worries of its own. There is no need to add to the troubles each day brings" (Matt. 6:34). We cannot cause yesterday's sun to rise again or hurry tomorrow's. The present moment is all we can ever hope to have, therefore we live in it and only it.

Healing and health require that we take some responsibility for our own well being. We cannot allow our imagination to run rampant. Every time we read about a disease or the symptoms we do not need to identify with it and claim it for ourselves. Some persons, through self-diagnosis become so certain that there is an illness that even the most trusted doctors have difficulty in disabusing them of the idea. People who continually talk about an illness invariably invite it. Thoughts tend to reproduce themselves in reality.

HEALING

In this same vein we do not accept a condition as final—terminal. A patient with a fast-growing malignancy said, "There is no longer an 'if' question. It is only 'when.' " Of course there was depression. All hope was gone. Rather than yielding to discouragement this is the time to affirm, "My help comes from the Lord, who made heaven and earth" (Ps. 121:2 RSV).

A doctor, whose specialty is cancer, said, "Upon a number of occasions I have said to the nurse, 'Make this patient as comfortable as possible. It is only a matter of hours.' Yet the next day that patient has greeted me with a cheery, 'Good morning,' and I have seen that one walk from the hospital."

If the patient is determined to live, the doctor has a strong ally in the work he or she is trying to do. Divine healing is the gift of God to the sufferer in need. It is through our faith that we allow him to accomplish his perfect will. We can, and should, pray for the healing of mind and body, but even more we should pray for the healing of spirit and soul. Whether it be for self or others, this is an opportunity we must accept. Never should we be discouraged if our first attempts at prayers for healing do not bring the desired results. For too long we have programmed our minds with the negative, yet there is no way of knowing how many healing prayers have been responsible for accomplishing miracles of healing. In praying for healing there must be more than mere words. There must be a sincere desire to absorb God's truth. This may mean total surrender, willingness to cooperate, even the determination to live one's life in an entirely new direction.

James has written, "This prayer made in faith will heal the sick person; the Lord will restore him to health, and the sins he has committed will be forgiven" (James 5:15).

Healing can only take place when faith makes room for it. To think upon the indwelling presence of the Christ is to

THE ONE YOU CAN BECOME

cause new life, new energy, to flow through our bodies with a stronger force than the one that is causing the suffering.

While there are many who have experienced spiritual healing, and know how it came to them, there are others who have experienced it and do not understand it. But there are also many who could be healed of their suffering if they were open to it. Here we have the freedom of choice. We can approach it with skepticism, give a careful intellectual glance at it, or we can yield to it with perfect confidence, saying, "Lord, I give this entire problem to you." Jesus said to the leper, "Your faith has made you well" (Luke 17:19).

In his writing, Paul Tournier emphasizes the difference between technical medicine and the medicine of the person. He tells us that more and more doctors are combining the two with far-reaching results. Marian, a longtime friend, has suffered so much from arthritis. She refused to shake hands because of the pain it caused. Her doctor had treated her with the best technical medicine at his command. On one of her visits to his office he said, "Marian, do you believe in prayer?" When she responded in the affirmative he said, "I have been praying for you. Medicine is not bringing the relief we had hoped. I am going to continue to pray for you, and I am going to ask you to pray in faith believing that you will experience relief from your pain and that you will be healed entirely."

For a moment Marian explained she was almost too surprised to answer. Then she said, "Doctor, I believe it can happen. We'll both pray."

And it did happen. Not a total cure as yet, but there has been so much relief from constant pain that she is carrying on with a normal, active life, taking trips, working in her church, caring for her home and garden.

Healing is the Spirit of the living God at work within us. The healing nature that is present in our bodies is the gift of God. Immediately when disease comes upon us or our body is wounded in some way, the healing forces go to work to

HEALING

restore it. Healing is as much a part of life as is breathing; yet too often these great forces are hindered by our negative thinking. We begin to worry, have doubts, question if we will ever be well again. We may even have doubts about God thinking that by our illness or an accident he is punishing us for something we have done. While it is true that by our own actions we may have brought this seeming misfortune upon ourselves, God does not use these means to punish us. Nothing has ever happened to indicate that God uses sickness or pain to punish anyone. In no way did Jesus ever point to this. Rather he was quick to forgive, quick to heal, quick to restore. He cares for all who come to him regardless of what they may have done. His nature, his love, is the same today as it was when he walked the earth in the flesh.

People often express the thought either in ordinary conversation or in their prayers that if it is God's will they will be healed. Again, this is a mistaken idea of an avenging God punishing a wayward child. Nothing could be further from the truth. If we are created in the spiritual image of God and his Spirit indwells within us, his only thought would be our perfect wholeness.

When it comes to divine healing, the big fault undoubtedly lies within ourselves. If we were more receptive to it, healing might take place more rapidly. Animals demonstrate this daily. A sick or injured animal seeks a secluded place and remains quiet until healing takes place. Blood coagulates, bones knit, muscles unite, skin grows. Of course a veterinarian might speed the process, often does by cleansing the wound, bringing broken bones and flesh together, prevents scarring, but that is as far as he or she can go. The healing is Life restoring life.

Never, however, would we claim that if we had perfect faith we would be cured of all pain and suffering. That would be a dangerous affirmation. To believe that healing depends solely on faith leads to the obvious conclusion that

THE ONE YOU CAN BECOME

if we had sufficient faith we would never die. Spiritual healing of the body is an act of God's sovereign grace administered by his Spirit and used for his glory.

Knowing this we give ourselves completely over to God's healing, forgiving, freeing, loving presence. We see ourselves as restored and in harmony with our Creator. We thank him that he surrounds us and infills us with his infinite peace, strength, energy, and harmony, that his power is with us to heal, and then we trust him for the perfect outcome.

Health and wholeness are a part of God's divine plan for his children, and so we affirm health. We claim it as our perfect right.

STAND FIRM

The antidote for fear is spiritual faith. Fear is everywhere until it has become a fixed way of life for millions. We live with a continual dread that something awful is going to happen: illness, loss of job, loss of money, fear that we will be assigned an impossible task, fear of those who might move into our neighborhood.

In his book *In Tune with the Infinite,* Ralph Waldo Trine has written, "Fear and lack of faith go hand in hand. The one is born of the other. Tell me how much one is given to fear and I will tell you how much faith he lacks."

The expressions "I am afraid" "I don't think I can," "But what if something happens?" are negative responses that have turned aside more opportunities for wholeness perhaps than any other utterances.

A pastor of a large, sophisticated, metropolitan church asked his congregation to pray for the healing of a member who was critically ill. The response was, "But supposing our prayers aren't answered, what will it do to this church?" They never learned because that negative voice predominated.

Courage comes from so rearranging our thinking and our reactions to life that we will draw on that infinite source of strength which is God.

That there is a vast difference between foolhardiness and spiritual courage few will deny. Foolhardiness is simply pushing our luck to the utmost, taking chances that the law

THE ONE YOU CAN BECOME

of averages will not catch up with us. Courage is faith so rooted in the presence of God that even though we walk through the valley of the shadow of death we will fear no evil.

If we look back to the founders of our nation, they were persons who had an unshakable faith in God that gave them the courage of their convictions. Great men and women, for the most part, have been those who have walked with God. History and the Bible testify to this.

Of all the great characters of the Bible perhaps none displayed greater courage and confidence in the face of physical danger and suffering than did the apostle Paul. Near the close of his life he could write to his young friend Timothy, "But I am still full of confidence, because I know whom I have trusted, and I am sure that he is able to keep safe until that Day what he has entrusted to me" (II Tim. 1:12).

As always the choice is ours. We can continue in our fears, or we can replace them with courage that comes through our understanding and accepting our oneness with the divine source of strength and his universe.

Talk with a group of letter carriers or meter readers. Those who report they are afraid of dogs can show numerous scars to prove their point; yet in the same group will be those who are quick to assert that dogs do not bother them because without flinching, they look fearlessly at the dog confronting them, speak a word of firmness, and go their way undisturbed.

However, there is an often overlooked fact; there is something stronger than physical courage—spiritual courage. When the spirit of the one with true spiritual courage meets the spirit of the one who does not have this type of courage, the outcome is generally already determined. Spiritual courage triumphs.

Today, perhaps one of the most prevalent places where courage is needed is for those who are facing loneliness. The pastor of a church of two thousand members who makes a practice of praying daily for certain of his parishioners sends out a questionnaire in advance stating that if there are special needs in the lives of those for whom he will be praying to indicate the needs. After long months of following this practice he has reported that 40 percent of the requests are for courage to face loneliness. This, he emphasizes, is not confined to any particular age group. While the elderly do have fears about their inability to care for themselves, teen-agers also express how greatly they are troubled by the feeling of loneliness, of having no one to whom they can turn with confidence.

Whether we are alone because we find ourselves in strange surroundings or because of broken families or when a loved one of many years has been taken from us, this is the time to turn more sincerely and more often to the comfort and stength by affirming that we are not alone, that the very presence of God is with us, to strengthen, to comfort, and to give direction.

We turn to him, not only knowing that he is with us, but we hand our suffering, our frustration, over to him by simply saying, "Father, this is too much for me. I am releasing it to you to be replaced by your Spirit." Then, after a moment of meditation on this fact, ask, "Now what can I do to help myself?" Pause and listen. Listen carefully. Very often we will be directed to one who is in greater need of comfort and understanding, or we will be directed to a worthwhile activity that will so completely absorb us that we will have little or no time to experience the sorrow and fear that comes with loneliness.

When we realize that God has accepted us, problem and all, not only accepted us, but that he is with us, it is easier to find others who will accept us, because having handed our problem over to him we do not feel the necessity of burdening others with it. We become the strong, radiant persons he intended us to be.

The psalmist who had faced many of the raw emotions of

THE ONE YOU CAN BECOME

life spoke of courage so many times. To repeat the first three verses of the Forty-sixth Psalm when nature goes on a rampage is to bring a calm and leave us free to direct our physical energies in the direction that will be most helpful.

A family camping in the Rocky Mountains in Montana at the time of the earthquake there that took so many lives tells of feeling the first terrifying tremors. For a moment they huddled together, then the father led them in the words: "God is our refuge and strength, a very present help in trouble. Therefore we will not fear though the earth should change, though the mountains shake in the heart of the sea; though its waters roar and foam, though the mountains tremble with its tumult" (Ps. 46:1-3 RSV).

Later the father said that that moment of trust calmed their fears and enabled them to act wisely so they lived and were able to tell about it.

The Ninety-first Psalm is a poem of the security of the godly. Sometimes it has been called the soldier's psalm. For the fearful there could be no better antidote than to memorize this psalm. There is so much assurance when the psalmist says, "For he will give his angels charge of you to guard you in all your ways" (Ps. 91:11 RSV).

Angels! Do we believe in angels? Jesus believed in them. The Bible speaks of them some three hundred times. In the first volume of his *Institutes of Christian Religion,* Calvin said, "Angels are the dispensers and administrators of the divine beneficence toward us. They regard our safety, undertake our defense, direct our ways, and exercise a constant solicitude that no evil befall us."

How many times, when in a moment of frivolity we have tried to explain a miraculous escape from apparent disaster, have we said, "My guardian angel must have been perched on my shoulder"? Perhaps there was more truth in that statement than we have realized.

Guardian angels, the presence of God, think of it as we will, we are surrounded by the Force of forces if we but accept reality. This assurance will bring courage to the fearful, calm frightened nerves, give stability to our emotions.

There are those times when fear becomes very real: when facing a serious operation, when caught in a storm, when financial disaster looms. These are times to face our fear squarely and proclaim "that God is our refuge and strength." We do not doubt, and we do not fear. The indwelling presence of God has control over all fear, over all situations with which we are confronted. With our faith secure in God we are not disturbed by outer appearances. We are a part of his great Oneness. His Spirit is our spirit. To be a child of God is to live in perfect confidence that he is our strength to meet any emergency.

A man in his late seventies, who underwent open heart surgery said before the operation, "I have no fear." Six weeks later, when he was walking one mile every morning he said. "I had no doubt about the outcome."

Faith in the presence of God enables us to stand firm when facing adverse circumstances. We remain confident in the knowledge that the mighty power of God is greater than any outward appearances.

When facing a new job, a move to a strange locality, an adverse financial situation, loneliness, pain, and having done all that we can to alleviate the situation we reread the account of the Children of Israel fleeing from Pharaoh and accept at face value the admonition, "Fear not, stand firm, and see the salvation of the Lord, which he will work for you today" (Exod. 14:13 RSV).

This is our answer to fear. We stand firm.

THE ONE YOU CAN BECOME

Thomas R. Kelley, in his essay "Holy Obedience," has written:

> The life that intends to be wholly obedient, wholly submissive, wholly listening, is astonishing in its completeness. Its joys are ravishing, its peace profound, its humility the deepest, its power world-shaking, its love enveloping, its simplicity that of a trusting child.

The apostle Paul, in his letter to the people at Philippi, wrote, "But whatever happens, make sure that your everyday life is worthy of the gospel of Christ" (Phil. 1:27 Phillips).

To become the one we might become depends upon our desire and our willingness to follow these precepts.

To arrive at this goal requires more than a theory, more than words in a book. There must come a time when each one of us becomes quiet and in the solitude of soul formulates the image we want of ourselves—the image we will be comfortable to live with and present to the world.

To study the Bible, even memorize it, is meaningless except for conversation unless we apply these precepts to all the challenges of life. While we may proclaim that we have faith, it is useless unless we practice it. In our development there comes a time when we have learned enough of the basics to start on the road of experience, then

THE ONE WE MIGHT BECOME

continue our learning from there, not neglecting our reading, our searching, but implementing it with reality until it becomes a way of life. If we do not do that, we find ourselves spending pleasant hours gathering a mass of information but without practical application or results.

Meister Eckhart wrote, "There are plenty to follow our Lord half-way, but not the other half."

To become requires that we go the full route with faith and self-discipline that leads to complete obedience without any reservation. This is when the indwelling Spirit breaks through, miracles become commonplace, divine forces are released, and we are changed persons.

At the mention of discipline, even self-discipline, however, there are those who shy away. Actual discipline means living up to certain guidelines that either we have established for ourselves or others have established for us. This is where Meister Eckhart's statement becomes too true. We believe in discipline only to that point where it begins to infringe on our own secret enjoyments and indulgences.

The person who enjoys sleeping until the last minute, then rushing to school or work does not want the discipline of arising a few minutes early for meditation and prayer to put the day in order. Such persons forget that when self is emptied into God and God infills us, these moments become the most delightful times of the day. It is here that God slips into our consciousness like a canoe slipping into a quiet lagoon and that his presence can be felt all day.

To pause at night, tired though we may be, and review the preceding day with God is to invite rest and protection, knowing that the morrow will be lived on a higher plane than the day just finished.

Faith and obedience were the life of the prophets, Jesus of Nazareth, the disciples.

In *The Simple Life,* Vernard Eller has written, "Jesus stakes his teaching of the simple life upon one and only one principle, namely that absolute personal loyalty to God must take precedence over anything and everything else."

Some years ago the late President Eisenhower wrote a heart-warming article, "The Day I Knew I Belonged to the Flag." In it he told of his first day at West Point and how as a new cadet when he saw the flag lowered for the evening he knew he belonged to it body and soul and would follow it to the end of his days.

To be faithful to self may mean forgetting the pleasure and temptations of the minute to reach a higher goal. To be faithful to others may mean the forgetting of self as others are benefited. To be faithful to God sometimes means walking that second mile because he first loved us, breathed the breath of life into our being, and now indwells within us where he will remain for all eternity. It is more than a mild veneer of religious respectability; it is a life of total obedience to his love. We are that child who holds out a hand to a beloved parent and says, "Help me," knowing that help and strength are forthcoming.

We stake our all on God's faithfulness, for he said, "I will never leave you; I will never abandon you" (Heb. 13:5).

Our faith in the Spirit of God that indwells within us does not relieve us of responsibility. Rather our oneness with him strengthens our efforts and makes us confident to act with enthusiasm and trust. We do not hesitate to make decisions, we are not afraid to venture out when the call comes. We do our absolute best to bring about rightness in our lives and the lives of those with whom we come in contact. We know, however, that greater than our human efforts God is at work, that his love and Spirit will bring forth results far beyond anything we might expect.

Here we come back to the statement of William James included earlier in this book: "The turning point in religious experience is self-surrender."

For the majority of us the word "surrender" is abhorrent. It was for me until I read Dr. Tournier's explanation: "For me,

THE ONE WE MIGHT BECOME

this surrender of my life to God has never meant that I was turning my back on the world—rather that I was interesting myself in it in a wider and deeper way. Nor did it mean, at that time, that I gave up action. What I was giving up was my claim to act in accordance with my own will, in order to allow myself to be led as much as possible by God."

Here we think of the well-known experience of E. Stanley Jones, who upon his decsion to become a missionary declared himself for Africa. Yet after a time of honest prayer he was to say, "It is India." From that vantage point he was to become missionary, evangelist, author, world traveler, and confidant of presidents and rulers.

True prayer begins in the heart as we realize the presence of God, takes shape in the mind, and finds expression in life. Thus we execute the fundamentals and come into harmony with the force that strengthens us to fulfill our highest potential.